TEACHING ACTING

SOME THINGS I LEARNED ALONG THE WAY

For Actors, Directors and Teachers

By
Anthony B. (Tony) Schmitt Jr.

Teaching Acting
Some Things I Learned Along the Way
For Actors, Directors and Teachers

By
Anthony B. (Tony) Schmitt Jr.

Copyright 2020 Anthony B. Schmitt Jr.
All rights reserved

Published on Lulu.com
Copies can be purchased online at lulu.com

Cover design by Robert J. Medici

DEDICATION

To my family, and especially to my father,
Anthony Bernard Schmitt Sr.

Thank you for encouraging me
to pursue my dreams.

Preface

Tony Schmitt spent his professional life teaching acting and directing plays mostly in educational theatre. When he was directing, he always felt that he was also teaching or coaching acting.

Tony completed this book shortly before he passed away. He worked on this book for several years; he consulted many people, friends, colleagues and former students, and he revised it several times. One of the last things we did together was to finalize the Table of Contents. I promised him that I would format and edit it, never thinking that he would not see the final copy. With the great help of Tony's good friend, John Gutting, I have tried to keep my promise.

I first saw Tony in *The Taming of the Shrew* at Xavier University in Cincinnati, Ohio, when I was in high school. I had no idea who he was or that we would ever know each other. (Tony and I were married in 1961.) We were introduced by his sister when we were in college and from that time on, I shared and saw almost all his theatre acting and directing experiences.

Over the years, he directed at least 100 fully-produced plays: at Otterbein College; Gannon College; University of Wisconsin-Stevens Point; Wayne State University's Hilberry, Bontstelle and Studio Theatres; the Attic Theatre in Detroit; the Utah Shakespeare Festival; Cherry County Playhouse in Muskegon, Michigan; Meadow Brook Theatre in Rochester, Michigan; and Shakespeare in the Park in Royal Oak, Michigan. I was always a very proud audience member.

He prepared for each of those productions and for all his many classes, each time, as though he were directing and teaching the material for the first time. Periodically I asked him why he had to prepare for a student's class scene which was from a play that he had both been in and directed. He said he just did.

He was respected by so many and I believe there was a reason for that: He was so passionate about his work and he cared about the many people with whom he worked and taught. As you read Tony's book, I hope you will see that passion about his work in acting, teaching and directing.

Quotes from two of his students:

"…. You get the basic physical stuff out of the way and start tweaking with timing, and refined blocking and just the heartbeat of it all. That's what I remember about your work...never really finished...always, always, looking for more, more; a moment...one more laugh...figuring out why one thing isn't working...and then how to make it work." (Thomas Nardone, M.A., M.S., *actor, director, teacher, Principal, Assistant Superintendent*)

"Honestly, you are the most instrumental teacher director I've ever had. You've helped shape my thoughts and beliefs about the art form and provided the best example of true professionalism." (Richard Gustin, M.F.A., *actor, director, playwright, producer, teacher*)

As I worked on this book, I could hear Tony's voice and his passion for what he had learned and what he believed. I guess I had absorbed more than I thought. He did always talk about his work and the work in the many plays and movies that we saw together over the years! I hope that those of you who knew him will hear that same voice and will know that he would be honored to know that you are reading this and sharing his life's work.

--Jan (Janet Barrett Moore Schmitt)

CONTENTS

Prologue 9

Part One: Internal Techniques

Chapter 1: What am I Doing? The Action 27

Chapter 2: What's in my Way? The Obstacle 39

Chapter 3: Real Thoughts, Vivid Images. 43
The Inner Monologue

Chapter 4: Talk *to* Other People, Not *at* Them. 51
Communication

Chapter 5: Coming Alive in the Presence of Your
Partner 57

Chapter 6: What Might it Be Like If? Imagination 65

Chapter 7: What Am I Feeling? Emotion 77

Part Two: External Techniques

Chapter 8: Look and See. Listen and Hear.
Observation 91

Chapter 9: What Happens in This Scene?
Tell the Story 97

Chapter 10: Who is This Person I Am? The Character 109

Chapter 11: Can I Be Heard? The Voice 117

Chapter 12: Can I Be Understood? Diction 125

Chapter 13: Playing the Music. Sense and Music
in the Language. Making your Points. 129

Chapter 14: Shaping the Performance.
Movement on Stage 135

Part Three: Other Useful Techniques and Exercises

Chapter 15: But It Should Be Fun. Letting Go.
Enjoying It All 145

Chapter 16: Other Useful Techniques 155

Chapter 17: Performance Sense 165

Chapter 18: Terminology 167

Chapter 19: Responding to a Scene or Monologue 169

Chapter 20: What is Acting? 173

Conclusion 179

Books I have Used and Recommend/*Credits* 187

Acknowledgements 191

About the Author/In Praise of Tony Schmitt 193

Index 197

PROLOGUE

A few years ago, I received an email from Chris Bohan, an actor I directed at The Hilberry Theatre at Wayne State University, who, after completing his MFA, took a part-time job at Lehigh University as an acting teacher. It was his first experience teaching, and although he was excited by this new adventure, he felt uneasy about it at the same time. He wrote:

> In one of your previous emails you had stated something to the effect that it took you a while to get in a groove as an acting teacher. And, I was hoping you could expand on what that meant. It seemed like you were saying that it took you a while to figure out what and how to teach acting. Is this correct?
> This semester I am teaching three classes: Acting 1, Acting 2, and a Character Development class. There have been days when I just don't feel comfortable in my classes. I feel there is something more I should be teaching them, something I am missing. I have several exercises I use, and I put a lot of emphasis on objective and actions and conflict. And, I am wondering...what else is there?
> I know that not all my students will turn out to be professional actors, but I still feel like I haven't reached my stride yet. I was just wondering if there is any guidance you could give to a novice teacher who really cares about his students, and who wants to make sure he is giving them the best guidance.

My response poured out in an almost startling way. I was excited by this opportunity to share with Chris some of the things I discovered in my 38 years of teaching, things I came to feel strongly about. It was sheer fun to offer him some techniques and ideas he might find useful, things I had enjoyed doing so much over the years. It was the beginning of an exchange of emails that I have enjoyed as he has grown as a teacher.

While communicating with Chris, I found myself forced to look back at my own evolution as a teacher of acting, and in the process, I relearned some things I had forgotten.

Like so many of us, I jumped into this work with the simple, zealous drive that it was something I just wanted to do. So, let me give you a thumbnail sketch of how this all came about.

In the spring of 1956, an article appeared in a Sunday edition of *The Cincinnati Enquirer* announcing the upcoming season of The Cincinnati Summer Playhouse. This theatre was a fully professional, star-system operation, housed in a tent, set in the round, and playing in weekly stock. The article displayed pictures of the stars who were prominent actors of the time such as Judith Anderson, Maureen Stapleton, Luther Adler, Joan Blondell, Eva Gabor, John Ireland, Caesar Romero, and many more. The article also mentioned the fact that the theatre was accepting applications for apprentices who would join the company and be paid a dollar a week for their efforts.

With the generous consent of my father, I applied for and was awarded an apprenticeship at the Playhouse. My excitement knew no bounds, but I was also very nervous about being a part of such a company. Would I be able to measure up? Could I function there among these seasoned professionals with their stellar credentials? I had only played the lead in my high school play and was not very well versed in the ways of the theatre. I was truly a babe-in-the-woods.

Shortly before I began my apprenticeship, an article appeared in *Theatre Arts* magazine which cautioned us apprentices about the reality of what to expect in our upcoming jobs. It informed us that our work would be unglamorous, dirty, demanding, rigorous, and even menial, like picking up the garbage, and it especially warned us not to expect to get onstage to act. So, I went to the Playhouse fully expecting to work hard and not to get on stage at all. But I was about to get my first eye-opening experience.

I arrived at the tented, big-top Playhouse and was met by the young, genial general manager, Doug Cramer, who eventually became the head of a Hollywood studio. He quickly introduced me to my new bosses, the resident set designer, a recent Yale graduate, and the union-man lighting technician, and off I went, nervously, to begin my work in the real theatre.

Early in the season, Luther Adler came through with a touring production of Arthur Miller's *A View from the Bridge*, in which Mr. Adler was the star as well as the director. Born into a family of celebrated actors, Adler had been a member of the famous Group Theatre of the 1930s, and he was a star of stage and screen, though I, of course, knew none of this.

I was given a walk-on role, one of three illegal aliens who were hiding out in Eddie Carbone's (Adler's) house, discovered by an immigration officer, and carted off to jail. In a brief rehearsal, Mr. Adler said, "All right, you, officer, bring them in down the 9-o'clock ramp, hit the stage, stop when you get on to it; you three (me and the other two) look at me, and then the officer takes you off the 12-o'clock ramp." We did it. Simple. I could handle that. Except...

On opening night, I did just what Mr. Adler said. I hit the stage, looked at him, and Kaboom! He looked back at me, terror in his eyes. Two hundred and twenty volts of electricity were coming at me, the magnetism of which simply yanked me into the real world of the play. I wasn't onstage anymore. I was in the room with this horrified man whose contact with me for that instant was intensely personal and compelling. I exited and then it hit me: "Oh, THAT'S what acting is!" It was my "Saint Paul on the road to Damascus" moment, when he was knocked off his horse by the divine.

Later in that season, despite the warning in *Theatre Arts* magazine, I actually had a small speaking role in *The Young and Beautiful* with Lois Smith, who had just come from doing the play on Broadway. Once again, the immediacy and real-life sense of what she was doing, making it genuine conversation, made it personal and pulled me in. I just went where her immediacy and personal connection took me. It didn't feel like a performance at all. We talked to each other on stage, we Castle Walked, and had great fun. And when she told me later, "You're a good Sonny Dorrance" (my character's name), I was over the moon.

I learned so much during the three seasons I spent at The Playhouse. I built sets and collected furniture props during the day, and I assisted the union technician running the light-board at night, where I watched the actors, night after night as they educated me: the musicality of Judith Anderson's dialogue in *Black Chiffon*, Signe Hasso's raw, animal energy as Anastasia, Maureen Stapleton's quiet complexity and immediacy in *The Lady of Larkspur Lotion* mesmerized me.

I also learned a lot from just talking with the resident and guest actors of the company. Despite my initial fear of not being accepted, these generous people were ready and willing to talk with a young apprentice about the craft of acting and their experiences in it. I watched how they went about their work, how they rehearsed, how they prepared. And they didn't treat me as the green kid I was, but as a member of the team who tried to contribute to the success of the show, as I hammered, sawed, hung and ran the lights, yes, and picked up the garbage.

Although they were fun-loving people, I saw that they were as serious about their work as my father was about his real estate business. Looking back on it, I realize that so much of how I view the process of doing theatre came from that experience at the Playhouse. Hearing the stage manager say, after we had to hold the curtain for 10 minutes and the audience started a rhythmic clapping, "God damn it! Now we've lost them!" The respect for the audience was all important. The same stage manager, asking the props girl, just before curtain time, "Did you check the props?" "Yes, Ed, I did." "Did you double-check the props?" "Yes, Ed, I did." "Then triple-check them."

While I spent my summers at the Playhouse, I continued my theatre training during the rest of the year at Xavier University. It was my very good fortune that at the very time of my entering, the university had just hired a new faculty member to head up the theatre program. His name was Otto Kvapil, a recent graduate of Catholic University's respected Theatre Department. He came in loaded with creative energy, devoted to the classics, particularly the comedies, superb directorial skills, and a hunger to do plays, plays, and more plays. His enthusiasm for the theatre and his infectious spirit drew many students to him. He had a twinkle in his eye, a sly smile, and a ready quip at the tip of his tongue, which had us all laughing almost constantly. We would follow him anywhere, and he began to put his mark on theatre at Xavier.

His first production was Shakespeare's *The Taming of the Shrew*. He cast me as Lucentio, the young romantic who arrives at Padua Nursery of Arts with his servant, Tranio, to whom he says, "Here let us breathe, and haply institute a course of learning and ingenious studies…" Under Otto's direction, I was indeed breathing the magical air of Padua, while my servant, Tranio, was leering at women as they wandered past. The taming scene between Petruchio and Kate was a laugh riot with all of Otto's comic invention released at its best. For example, Kate hauled off and smacked Petruchio who tromped on her foot as he said, "Oh, let me see thee walk!" The sell-out audience loved it!

One of the most important things I learned from Otto was his ability to take classical characters and turn them into contemporary people with all the recognizable comic foibles that made them appealing. Under his direction, the plays leapt to life, as all the characters up on stage became real human beings, clearly defined, who advanced the story of the play. The people of Shakespeare, Moliere and Wilde were loveable, laughable, quirky individuals who delighted the audience.

The theatre training at Xavier was largely experiential, consisting of performance work on stage in front of sizeable audiences, presenting classical material, under the guidance of a gifted director. In this context the audience was my ultimate teacher. I learned firsthand how a moment of forced performance could kill a laugh, or how true honesty in acting could draw an audience into the world of the play and tell its story.

I learned so much under Otto's direction. His encouragement, sense of fun, keen directorial eye, and the good roles he cast me in, gave me a sense of confidence that was energizing and liberating. As I worked in theatre over the years, I realized over and again how much his influence affected me.

Otto was a true mentor whose house became a gathering place for the theatre students. Evenings there with him and his wife, Diane, herself a graduate of The Neighborhood Playhouse, were filled with laughter, imitations of each other and people we knew, improvisation scenes, and a constant, "Can you top this?" string of comic tales and quips. I painted his house, others babysat his kids, some roomed in his house, and became a part of his family. I was so attracted by his work and lifestyle that my fantasy was to have a job, a situation just like his, where I could direct plays and teach theatre classes.

In my last year at Xavier, I was accepted as a graduate assistant, in the Theatre Department at Saint Louis University with a scholarship for studies leading to a Master of Arts in Theatre, a package that included graduate theatre classes, technical work in the theatre's ambitious production program, acting in the productions, and teaching basic public-speaking courses. It was my first opportunity to immerse myself totally in the study and practice of theatre. The classes, taught by a top-notch faculty, opened my eyes to the range of dramatic literature and theatre history. The high-quality production work afforded me an opportunity to continue and extend my acting skills, and the speech classes became my initiation to the world of teaching. I loved it.

Following the completion of my Masters' work at St. Louis U., I spent two years fulfilling my military obligation in the Army and a year teaching high school English, after which I was offered and accepted a faculty position at Gannon College in Erie, Pennsylvania. The position was for a teacher of a required Public Speaking course and a director of the Theatre Program. The latter included directing whatever plays I chose, teaching the few theatre courses on the books, and managing the theatre building, the original Erie Playhouse.

With very little directing experience to my credit, I plunged in, directing four shows a year. I had to learn rather quickly how to stage a play, block it, invent business that would tell the story and keep it interesting. In the process I discovered how the creation of the most effective physical activity led the actors to perform more truthfully and believably. Of course, I was aware of this in my own acting, but now, having the responsibility of the production, I saw the vital necessity of this technique to bring the show fully to life, grab the audience's attention, and hold it.

I encouraged the actors to actually talk to each other on stage (thank you, Lois Smith), and to make dynamic connections with each other (thank you, Luther Adler) to interfere with each other, and to compete. I also urged them to create their own physical actions, and I observed that, when they did own these, the actions were the most effective.

Inspired by Moss Hart's, *Act One,* I became an avid audience watcher, looking for any signs of inattention—the bobbing leg, the glance at the watch, etc., signs that our work was not compelling or holding an audience's attention. These were almost always the result of acting or directing problems.

I also began my teaching of acting classes in Erie. Having no experience in this, I sought the help from any book on the craft that I could lay my hands on, but I found myself coming back again and again to Constantin Stanislavski's *An Actor*

Prepares. I had pored over this book in the past, and it had become my bible of acting books. And when I discovered Charles McGaw's *Acting is Believing*, which to my mind was a teaching or learning manual for *An Actor Prepares*, I seized on it. Basing his book on the techniques that Stanislavski laid out in his book, McGaw created exercises in each of them, for example: relaxation, concentration, objectives, observation, and so on.

Ultimately the scene work that the students performed in class became the culmination of Stanislavski's principles realized in performance, and I particularly stressed the technique of communion, which pushed them into vital connections with each other.

My experience at Gannon convinced me that college teaching, particularly in the area of theatre, was a career path that I wanted to continue, but to do this I would have to get a Ph.D. degree. To this end, I received a generous offer from The Ohio State University with its outstanding faculty, challenging academic program and extensive, excellent production work.

The depth of the Theatre History program, with its world-class collection, opened my eyes to a world of the theatre's past and its influence on the present. In dramatic literature and criticism, I was introduced to classic playwrights that were new to me, as well as concepts of theatre that awakened and challenged my thinking.

In spite of the heavy academic workload, I was able to continue my acting work at O.S.U.—work that gave me opportunities to appear in elaborately produced major productions, act in a world-premiere of a Jerome Lawrence and Robert E. Lee play, do a Harold Pinter play directed by a woman who had written a book on the author, and participate in other performance experiences that deepened my acting range.

I also taught acting at O.S.U., still using McGaw's book to provide the basic structure for the class, and kept my hand in directing, staging a major production at nearby Otterbein College.

After I completed my Ph.D. work, I took a job at the University of Wisconsin-Stevens Point. The Theatre Department there consisted of 10 faculty members, three of whom were in dance. My assignment as "the new man" was to teach the acting courses—my dream come true.

I quickly realized that to teach the various courses in acting, I would have to broaden the variety of my teaching techniques and expand my list of exercises in each of the basic elements of the craft. I gathered all the books I could find to help me with this—Lee Strasberg for relaxation and public solitude (the private moment exercise), Sonia Moore for inner monologue and justification, Uta Hagen for sense memory and objectives, Michael Chekhov for the imaginary body, Viola Spolin for improvisation in the "where" and a sense of place, and Stanislavski for characterization.

I also invented my own exercises in all the elements, particularly ones geared to coaxing partners to open up to each other, and truly communicate.

The students responded very positively to this work; there was some real learning going on, and we all had a great deal of fun. And yet I felt that something was still missing at the very core of the work, that something else needed to happen. I felt as if I were a painter standing in front of a big canvas, but I was just working at one little corner. That feeling was most noticeable when the students did their work on scenes.

I considered the work on text to be at the very heart of what we were doing. I gave my notes after each scene was presented, and then I would "work" on them, and this is where I used improvisation most effectively. To get at what might be lacking in a scene, I would force adjustments—whispered directions to one of the partners such as an added word or phrase to force inner monologue, a disagreement (obstacle) to vitalize an objective, questions to energize the communication.

These techniques were productive, bringing scenes alive and improving them, but I was still left with a desire to do something more central to what we were doing. And then one day....

Two young women were to do the tea scene from *The Importance of Being Earnest*. Just as Gwendolyn came on stage, before a word was spoken, I stopped her and said, "Liz, what are you doing?" It just popped out of my mouth. No plan at all. She said, "I'm coming on stage." I said, "No. What are you doing?" She said, "I'm thinking of a garden." I said, "I know why you said that, but Gwendolyn is already in the garden. So, what are you doing?" And we went from there. Kaboom! In that moment, another "Saint Paul on the road to Damascus" moment, my teaching took a decided step forward. I kept asking the same questions. "What are you doing? Why are you here? What did you come here to do? And when you see Cecily and start to encounter her, and she stands up to you, what are you doing? What do you need to get from her? What might it look like if you get it? For that matter, what am I (Tony) doing right now? What might it look like if I get it? And it's not all about ME, but what YOU do. I get it from YOU. Something I can see the result of." I had used the word "objective" a lot before and worked with it, but it now felt too technical and analytical. "No, WHAT THE HELL ARE YOU DOING? You, Gwendolyn, are looking through your lorgnette at Cecily, but what are you doing? Your eyes are bad? What are you doing to Cecily? You are examining her like a lab experiment. You need her to knuckle under and cede you all the power. You will know that when you see it from her. Is it in your consciousness? No, but it is down there in your gut. We see in Act One how you control and dominate people to get your own way. Why do you NEED it? Your whole life at this moment centers around marrying Earnest (Jack). Cecily is a threat to that as you see it. What's in the way of your getting what you need? Cecily is standing her own ground. She is not giving in at all. So, what do you do to get what you need…from the other person?"

Shortly after I made this discovery in my teaching, the book *Audition* by Michael Shurtleff came out. One of his "twelve guideposts to acting" asks the question "What are you fighting for?" That seemed to support what I was trying to do, that is, to find the most active, energizing, doable thing to...well...*do*. Later, *A Practical Handbook for the Actor* was released, and it too centered on the basic need for an actor to "find an action," guided by its nine qualities. The authors used the term "essential action" for the goal (objective) that the character is driven to pursue. I believe that the word "action" was what the members of the Group Theatre used for "objective." I liked it and used it myself. (Terminology is a problem I will deal with later). This discovery adjusted my approach to my teaching and formed a basis for my work going forward.

In my eighth year at U.W.S.P., I got a call from a former student, Dick Gustin, who, after his graduation, was accepted into the nationally renowned Hilberry Graduate Repertory Theatre Company of Wayne State University in Detroit. Dick was calling to tell me that a faculty member had suddenly died, and the Theatre Department was searching for a replacement. He thought I'd be good for the job, said he'd put in a good word for me, and that I should apply. I did apply, and was offered the job, a dream one, but a scary one, too.

Theatre at Wayne, with its national reputation, was a very heavily production-oriented program. Its flagship was the 500-seat Hilberry Theatre, which essentially functioned as a regional theatre. The company was made up of 50 M.F.A. and Ph.D. students in the various areas of production, 20 of whom were actors. All the company members were on full scholarships, and the acting company was very impressive. Many of them were mature and experienced (the oldest member was 52), and most went on to have successful professional careers.

The thrust of the training was essentially a learn-by-doing approach, with most of the actors' time being spent in rehearsal and performance, and there were classes in performance and academics as well. The program mounted seven productions in a season, many of which were drawn from the classics, totaling 150 performances.

The Hilberry had been established in 1963, with the encouragement and guidance of Tyrone Guthrie, who believed that the best way for an actor to learn his craft was, as he said, "To play the great concertos." The result of this approach was an impressive list of alumni, including Jeffrey Tambor, Max Wright, Ruben Santiago-Hudson, Phyliss Sommerville, and many others. It also enjoyed the strong support of a subscription-based audience from the greater-Detroit area.

In addition to the graduate program, the large undergraduate program produced six shows in a 1,200-seat proscenium space, plus three studio theatres. This program also had its list of outstanding alums, such as Barbara Tarbuck, Lily Tomlin, S. Epatha Merkerson, and many others.

The three studio theatres also produced many student productions and acting recitals. Opportunities for acting, directing, and design work abounded.

As a new member of WSU's ambitious theatre training program, I was immediately assigned to teach acting to the junior class. The focus for acting students in their third year, was on styles, and my job was to teach *Commedia del Arté*.

This was the beginning of my teaching a wonderful array of acting classes from many periods and styles, including contemporary works. I taught students on all levels from freshmen to graduate students, and in time I became head of the graduate acting program.

I spent 24½ years teaching and directing at Wayne State. So, what did I learn in all that time that affected my work? Well, to begin with, I came into a situation that was, as I mentioned, heavy on production. With the five theatres churning out production after production, there was so much work to be seen. I admired the performance work of so many of the actors both in the graduate and undergraduate theatres, but I felt that what I might contribute was to try to make sure that all the work was as grounded in truth as it could be. And to that end, I continued to develop and strengthen the techniques that I had begun to believe in when I was in Wisconsin.

The selection and pursuit of an action was paramount, and for a few years I borrowed Michael Shurtleff's, "What am I fighting for?" as a way to express and direct it. In time, I simply called it "the action," but the basic concept was the same. My focus was on having the scene become a living, breathing experience that would draw in and arrest the audience's attention. I wanted to make sure that the actors were *talking to* each other and *affecting* one another, that they were actually *dealing* with the obstacles that the other people in the scene presented, and that there were real things happening rather than the mere performance of dialogue.

I learned more and more to trust my own responses to the scenes I was watching in the classroom or in rehearsal, knowing that if my attention was wandering, so would the audience's. If I was watching *the performance* as opposed to being engaged, I had to find ways to bring it alive. I also became more and more committed to script work in class as opposed to lots of time spent on exercises, games, and improv, though I did use some of those techniques as well in class and even as a part of rehearsal, if the need arose. But it was important for me to be sure the actors knew what was happening in the script as a basis for choices they would eventually make. So, knowing what was happening in the script became an important element of the work, not as an academic exercise, but as a means of making the acting active.

What follows here are some of the ways I went about doing that. I make no claim to this being the only way, but simply one that worked for me, most of the time. I also found that actors were quite willing to embrace this kind of work and enjoyed doing it.

So, what did I tell Chris Bohan in response to his need to make his teaching more effective and give the students the best help he could give them? I urged him to lead his students toward acquiring measurable, definable skills. I recommended that he use scripted-material monologues to get things started and then scenes, augmented with specifically targeted exercises. I suggested that he begin by going to the core of the work by teaching this technique of *action*, and then apply it to scripted material. To do that, I laid out eight questions that an actor can ask herself as she searches for that perfect action. Let's lay out the questions and then apply them to a scene.

"THE YOUNG AND BEAUTIFUL"
Cincinnati Summer Playhouse

Otto Kvapil
Theatre Director
Xavier University
Cincinnati, Ohio

Tony Schmitt as Lucentio
The Taming of the Shrew
Xavier University

Tony Schmitt as Algernon with
Elizabeth Dammerall in
The Importance of Being Earnest
Xavier University

Tony Schmitt, Jean Tarrant
The Glass Menagerie
Erie Playhouse
Directed by Edward Graczyk

Tony Schmitt, David Ayers
The Night Thoreau Spent in Jail
World Premiere
The Ohio State University

Tony Schmitt as Henry Higgins
My Fair Lady
The Ohio State University

Bruce Vilanche, Tony Schmitt
My Fair Lady
The Ohio State University

PART ONE
INTERNAL TECHNIQUES

CHAPTER ONE
WHAT AM I
(THE CHARACTER) DOING?

The Action

This means exactly what it says. Something active, something pursuable, something you can see the result of, like we do in life (usually instinctively), what you want to *have happen*.

- Why am I doing this? To what end?

- Why do I need it?

This is often referred to as "What do I want?" but I like the sense of need because it has the potential of making it more dynamic and personal.

- What might it look like if I get it?

There's not only one answer to this question. The actor will imagine for herself what it might be, but it forces her to be specific and it generates a sense of reality as well.

- What's in the way?

Theatre is conflict, which generates tension and moves the play forward. What can go wrong?

- **What happens if I don't get it?**

Why does it matter? Why is it important? Why don't I just quit? Leave? Shut up? Why must I pursue it?

- **How will I know if I get it?**

It is almost always in the response of the other person. It's why I contend that the scene is almost always about the other person.

- **Do I get what I need or don't I?**

The test is in the other person's response.

It is important to stress at this point that the use of the eight questions is actor homework and not usually in the consciousness of the character when she is encountering the other person in the scene.

Now let's try applying these questions to the climactic scene of *The Diary of Anne Frank* (the original version by Goodrich and Hackett)

The Frank and Van Daan families and a friend, Mr. Dussel, have been in hiding from the Nazis in Amsterdam during World War II. Their hideout is a cramped set of three rooms over a warehouse. They have been kept alive by a friend, Miep, who had been bringing them food and supplies on an almost daily basis, but now, after two years, she has not shown up for three days. The tension has mounted for the people in hiding. Prior to this final scene, Mr. and Mrs. Van Daan, out of their sheer terror, have a huge fight, accusing each other of their present predicament. Their teen-age son, Peter, rushes to his room. Mr. and Mrs. Frank's teenage daughter, Anne, pursues him and goes into his room.

Anne
Look, Peter, the sky. What a lovely day. Aren't the clouds beautiful? You know what I do when it seems as if I couldn't stand being cooped up for one more minute? I think myself out. I think myself on a walk in the park where I used to go with Pim. Where the daffodils and the crocus and the violets grow down the slopes. You know the most wonderful thing about thinking yourself out? You can have it any way you like. You can have roses and violets and chrysanthemums all blooming at the same time.... It's funny.... I used to take it all for granted...and now I've gone crazy about everything to do with nature. Haven't you?

Peter
I've just gone crazy. I think if something doesn't happen soon...if we don't get out of here...I can't stand much more of it!

Anne
I wish you had a religion, Peter.

Peter
No, thanks. Not for me.

Anne
Oh, I don't mean you have to be Orthodox...or believe in heaven and hell and purgatory and things...I just mean some religion...it doesn't matter what. Just to believe in something! When I think of all that's out there...the trees...and flowers...and seagulls...when I think of the dearness of you, Peter...and the goodness of the people we know...Mr. Draler, Meip, Dirk, the

vegetable man, all risking their lives for us every day...when I think of these good things, I'm not afraid any more. ...I find myself, and God, and I...

Peter

That's fine! But when I begin to think, I get mad! Look at us, hiding out for two years. Not able to move! Caught like...waiting for them to come and get us...and all for what?

Anne

We're not the only people that've had to suffer. There've been people that've had to...sometimes one ...sometimes another...and yet

Peter

That doesn't make me feel any better!

Anne

I know it's terrible, trying to have any faith...when people are doing such horrible things...but you know what I sometimes think? I think the world may be going through a phase, the way I was with Mother. It'll pass, maybe not for hundreds of years, but some day...I still believe in spite of everything, that people are really good at heart.

Peter

I want to see something now...Not a thousand years from now.

Anne
But, Peter, if you'd only look at it as part of a great pattern... Listen to us, going at each other like a couple of stupid grown-ups! *(She holds out her hand to him. He takes it.)* Look at the sky now. Isn't it lovely? *(Peter stands behind her with his arms around her. They look at the sky.)* Someday, when we're outside I'm going to... *(the sound of a car outside, its brakes squealing as it comes to a sudden stop...sound of heavy boots on the into the door. The Nazis burst in.)*

Exercise: Now let's apply the questions to Anne:

What is she doing? It's obvious that she's trying to pull Peter out of his despair.

Why is she doing this? Whereas the first question is very clear from what the playwrights give her to say in the script, the "why" now begins to become partly an actor's choice. The relationship between Anne and Peter in the script suggests that they care about each other. She has just witnessed the horrible scene between Peter's parents, and she sees the great pain and fear in him as he goes off to his room. Does she believe that she is the one person in the room who must help him now, and relieve him of his despair? Does she fear that she may make it worse by trying to do this? Is she afraid that Peter might go off the deep end in a way that might endanger them all?

What does she need in this scene? The actor looks at the prior events of the play, particularly Anne's relationship to Peter, and decides how she feels about him. Is he really the closest friend she has in this group? Does she love him? What is her view of him? Of them? Is it the depth of her feeling for him that propels her to pursue him and try to pull him out of this awful state? What does she get out of it? That he shows some affection for her? Must she save him? For him? For her? These are some possible and personal things the actor will have to decide for herself.

What might it look like if she gets what she's after? Would Peter come out of his despair, become more positive, loosen up...maybe he'd even smile, or show signs of love? Would he calm down? Would he become his old self?

What's in the way of her getting it? This is obvious in the script. Peter counters every argument she sends out: the beautiful things outside, religion, the wonderful people we know, and his own emotional state. Peter is irritated with her happy talk.

How will she know if she gets it? If he is able to let go of some of his despair. The test is in him.

What happens if she fails at this? What can go wrong? Why doesn't she just leave? Go back to her room? Does she think his despair could ruin him? That he could endanger the whole group? Can she live with him in this condition? Is she the only one who can save him?

Does she get what she needs or not? She does. Peter puts his arms around her. She can talk freely again and share some humor with him, "Look at us going on like stupid grownups." It becomes personal again.

Exercise: What is Peter's action in this scene? Answer the same questions for him.

Here are additional questions (and answers) about this technique.

Okay, so why start with **"What am I doing?"**

- It is a very learnable, teachable skill.

- It is at the very core of the work. What the character is doing at this moment in the scene is the most basic thing that the actor can address. It drives the action of the play and moves it forward.

- By giving the actor something to do, it can free her up to immerse herself in the world of the play, and to avoid the trap of self-focus. It is such an easy thing for an actor to slip into performing and focusing (even subconsciously) on her acting, for example, "What are my hands doing?" "Do I look stupid?" "Am I believable?" "Am I hitting the emotional highs?" or focus on the performance aspects of the scene, rather than living the life of the character in the moment.

- It can begin to address the challenges of concentration, relaxation, and connection with her partner on stage.

- Isn't that what we do in life? Try using the technique of observation on yourself and see what happens. Think back on an encounter with another person, and then see if you didn't have a goal or desired outcome in mind when you were in it, maybe not consciously, but it was probably there. How were you hoping the other person would respond?

- Many other teachers and actors have stressed the importance of this skill. Sanford Meisner begins his book with the simple, direct statement "Acting is Doing." Annette Bening, in a TV interview, talked about her teaching and stated the three basic questions for an actor to answer: What am I doing? What do I want? What's in my way? Lloyd Richards is quoted as asking his actors, "What are you doing?" and "Why?" William Redfield in *Letters from an Actor*, in response to some actor's question, "Can't we just do it?" he says, "Do what?" Examples abound.

Some traps/dangers in pursuing this approach/skill:

- These "actions" usually happen in the gut (subconsciously) rather than consciously. Anne Frank probably doesn't go into Peter's room thinking "Now my goal here is..." But she does have a goal, because she keeps adjusting to each of Peter's objections, and, in fact, does get what she needs (wants) when she extends her hand to him.

- The actor will probably have to consciously choose the action (at least in her training) even though the character is not consciously choosing it. It's part of her homework, if you will. So how does this work? The actor does her homework at home and leaves it there. And when she comes to rehearsal, she connects with her partner and "plays the game." A sports analogy example: The Detroit Tigers once had a third baseman who was having trouble making accurate throws to first base, so, because he was such a good hitter, they made him a first baseman. The coach said that it would take him most of the season to learn the choreography of playing first base, so that the moves were instinctual rather than mental; that is, it needed to be in his gut.

- A technique such as this is not an end in itself, but merely a tool to aid the actor in the work he is doing. He uses the tool if or when he needs it. The beginning actor will probably need to work on it consciously to have the skill at his disposal. Ideally, in time, as he grows in his craft, he uses this skill without thinking about it (unless he gets in trouble). I had an actor friend who once said, "I want to learn all the techniques and then forget about them." Probably a worthy goal, but that usually takes time.

- Don't let the fact that you are trying to get something from another character cause you to stare unceasingly at her. Again, check how you do this in life.

- I found that terminology counts for a lot in this. I was more successful in asking an actor, "What are you doing?" rather than, "What is your objective?" The former seemed more like-life, and the latter seemed more technical and analytical. And I named the thing you are doing as "the action." As I said earlier, I chose that term because I believe it's what they called it in the Group Theatre.

Examples of Actions

A few examples of how the use of action can work in performance:

- In a production of *The Diary of Anne Frank* which I directed, the actor playing Anne was quite good and very suitable for the role. Her work was alive, honest, and she connected beautifully with the other characters in the play, but when she got to that last scene (the one cited above), things changed a bit. She began to speak in an elevated tone, and underlined the heroic qualities of Anne, all of which tended to draw our attention to her acting, which was not at all phony, but in a very odd way pulled us out of the world of the play as we watched her perform. So, I asked her, "Mary Ann, what are you doing here?" She said, "I am trying to get Peter out of his depression." I said "Ok, just do that." And Bingo! She did it. We were pulled back into the play.

- An actor playing Emily in *Our Town* did the same thing in her final farewell to the things of the world before she goes back to her grave. "…goodbye to clocks ticking, the smell of fresh sheets…Oh earth you are too wonderful…" The language got painted with a sense of great importance, and it called attention to itself. I said to the actor, "Katie, just say goodbye to the world. You are never going to see it again." And again, Bingo! She did it. It was much more affecting, made the play come alive, and she did it immediately without any discussion.

- I was acting in a production of Harold Pinter's *The Lover*, a play about a staid, traditional English couple who had dual identities. They had invented wildly erotic characters for themselves who would meet in the afternoons and have wild sexual flings and then return in the evenings to their staid lives. I was acting up a "Pinter storm," when the director said to me, "You do know he's jealous, don't you?" Well, no, I didn't know that. But once she said that, Bingo! I had something to do. Blow up the game. Destroy it by letting one life bleed into the other. My wife wanted to keep the game the same, so she turned on the sex, and guess what? She won.

- In the balcony scene of *Romeo and Juliet*, Romeo says, "O, wilt thou leave me so unsatisfied?" Juliet responds, "What satisfaction canst thou have tonight?" (The double entendre usually gets a laugh.) But Romeo tells her exactly what his action is when he replies with, "The exchange of thy love's faithful vow for mine." Isn't he really saying, "I have told you that I love you; aren't you going to say that you love me?" He has professed his love over and over, and now he *needs* to hear it from her, since he has been pressing her to do just that.

All of this is not to suggest that acting is all in your head. If anything, having and pursuing an action should help you avoid "head acting." It can free you from the focus on yourself on stage, and it will pull you into the world of the play where real people do real things. But how do you do that? Well, it begins with the vital and open connection you have with your partner.

CHAPTER TWO

WHAT'S IN THE WAY OF MY GETTING WHAT I NEED? WHAT'S STOPPING ME?

The Obstacle

A man goes to climb a mountain and he does. There is no drama in that. No tension, no conflict. Hardly a play.

In an interview, Arthur Miller stated the generally held concept that conflict is at the heart of drama. The resultant struggle propels the action forward. The character needs something that she cannot walk away from, and she must overcome whatever is in the way of satisfying that need. The actor must identify this obstacle and then work to overcome it. When put into action, this technique has the benefit of focusing the actor's work as well as freeing her up to avoid that old bugaboo of self-focus. It also has the benefits of moving the play forward, energizing the acting, and bringing the play to life.

For example, Anne Frank is compelled to pull Peter out of his despair, and she uses various ways try to do that: urging him to see the positive things in life, offering religion as a means to that end, appealing to the feeling that they have for each other, and the like. What's obviously in her way is the fact that Peter, in his despair, vigorously rejects each of these attempts. Her positive views of life get under his skin, and he forcefully rejects them. She must battle against these rejections as she tries to rescue him from his depression.

In my teaching, I discovered that urging acting students to embrace these struggles and to *go for it* in their work was very effective. Students took to it immediately. One of the ways we did this was by using monologues. I assigned monologue work early in the course to begin the work while they were preparing scene work with their partners. My beginning idea was that there really was no such thing as a monologue. So-called "monologues" were really dialogues with the self or with someone else. After the actor first presented his monologue, we determined what the action was, to whom he was speaking, and why he was doing that. Then I would pull another student aside to be his scene partner and whisper something in her ear about how she might respond to his monologue. She then became the "obstacle character" and might interrupt, be inattentive, preoccupied, not comprehend, be hurt, elated or exhibit any of a wide range of other emotional responses.

For example: One actor was doing the speech of the Dauphine from Shaw's *Saint Joan* in which he is talking to Joan about why he was not going to give her the resources she was asking for to battle the English. After his initial presentation of the monologue, which he "performed," we added a spunky Joan who challenged him verbally, which caused him to stand up for himself and go to battle with her. Suddenly the scene leapt to life, was comic as well as touching, and full of energy. This was essentially an improvisation, but the Dauphine did not change a word of his dialogue. Only the inner workings changed.

In another example, one student was doing a monologue from Goldoni's *The Liar* in which a father berated his son for his wanton ways to get the kid to change his behavior. I had the kid gradually ignore the father, walk away from him, shake his head as he almost laughed at it all. The effect was to have the actor playing the father pursue him all over the room, voice raising, tossing furniture aside, attacking the kid emotionally. Once again, the combat energized the scene and brought it totally to life, simply by giving the father a real obstacle to push against. The monologue thus became totally believable, totally honest, and totally engaging. And it was genuinely fun and engaging to watch.

Not all scenes are scenes of open combat or obvious outward struggle as in *The Liar* or *Saint Joan*. What about the famous drugstore scene from *Our Town* between George and Emily? What is George's action? And what is his obstacle in the scene? In the scene immediately before the one in the drugstore, Emily calls George out for being conceited, and tells him that the other girls have been talking about it. George is taken aback and invites Emily to have a soda with him at the drugstore where he hopes to win back her friendship.

What is in the way is Emily's attitude toward him, which he must change. As the scene progresses, he wants to take the relationship farther, but again he comes up against an obstacle: In his gut drive to get closer to Emily, he runs the risk of losing her. And so, he must inch forward, as he is impelled to deepen the connection with her without messing it up by assuming too much about her feelings toward him. And in the world of that play, a young man like George just didn't say, "Hey Emily, I really love you" even if that was on his mind. The perceived obstacle energizes the scene and pulls it forward.

Now be careful. As with so many of these techniques, there are potential traps along the way, and one of them is to "play" the technique (the obstacle) without grounding it in the action that is its animating force. Don't be seduced into making it all about the fight for its own sake without providing the underlying foundation for the fight. The fighting can feel good, but it is always a means to an end. Chris Bohan told me that his students at one point kept playing the obstacle rather than the action. To repeat myself, these techniques are *means*, not *ends*. No technique is an end in itself; it's only a way to get there.

A word about terminology: "Obstacle" is a handy technical term, and I kept using it. The more human, real-life way of using the concept is by asking, "What is in my way?" "What's stopping me?" If it's nothing, then the man climbs up the mountain without any problem or resistance. Not drama. Often the playwright will supply the conflict for the actor, and make it clear, but sometimes it is not obvious, in which case the actor will have to dig for it. Is it in the events of the play? The other character? Or even within himself? I once heard someone say,

"I have to have a conversation with myself about this problem." There can be two people inside one person who have contradictory views. Let them battle it out. Or the actor might use the audience to help him out here. Hamlet's "To be or not to be" soliloquy can be addressed to the crowd. To what end? (action) Is there something in the way? Might they be shaking their heads no while he contemplates suicide? Or might they be stunned that he would even consider that? Or might they be put off by him? Choices! Choices!

CHAPTER THREE

REAL THOUGHTS, VIVID IMAGES

The Inner Monologue

The wonderful actor Barry MacGregor of the Canadian Shaw and Stratford Theatre Festivals directed Alan Ayckbourn's *A Chorus of Disapproval* at the Hilberry Theatre. The production was a huge success, and the work of the actors was superb. It was compelling, alive, in-the-moment, true to life and wildly comical. I asked Barry how he got these terrific performances out of the actors, and he said, "I would not let them *speak* unless they had an *idea* in their heads." As far as I know, he simply gave that direction, and they just did it. He claimed that working in the plays of Shaw led him to this conclusion. He also said that he called out the actors on their "little tricks" when "performance" might substitute for real thought.

When I was directing *Auntie Mame*, I gave the leading lady a note saying that she lost me in a certain big speech. Her reply was: "Oh, my mind went to Toledo then." So, she knew exactly what the problem was and fixed it. No further discussion. No more mental trips to Toledo.

Simon Callow, in a TV interview, said that a major focus of his acting was "finding and thinking the actual thoughts of the character."

In my directing experience, I cannot begin to count the times I would say to an actor, "That moment right there was truly electric and compelling," and the actor would often reply, "Oh, that was when I forgot my line." Now what does that say? To me, when the actor couldn't remember his canned words, he was forced to come up with his own, which sounded more authentic, so at that moment, there was a mental energy that, as actors, we'd like to have all the time. Or as a certain English director said, "I want to see those ideas snapping off the stage!" And our ideas usually come fast and at times furiously. If the actor goes too slowly for too long, it is hard to follow. A paradox.

We humans cannot speak without an idea in our heads, unless we've memorized something, as actors must do. Then it is possible to do something that real people can't and don't do—speak without some kind of a mental track. In a way, actors live their acting lives backwards. They begin with a final result, that is, the script. Then they must try to go back to the mental and emotional source that triggered those words. Or, they can just "perform" the words, a subject we will consider later.

What's true of thoughts is also true of the images we often have in our heads as we speak. They too are a part of the mental track. I saw a brilliant example of this when I was watching Uta Hagen teach an acting workshop. In responding to a scene that she had just watched, she tried to offer a technique for an actor to use at a particular point, and she said, "It's as if you would say…" Then she stopped and said, "Wait I have to get my image." She paused and then, speaking as the character in the scene, she said, "Oh, do you mean that I got the part?" The line simply jumped to life. The surprise, the vulnerability, the joy, the immediacy, were all right there. It became a vivid example of what acting at its best can be, and all because of that image she consciously found and used.

Now, is all this necessary? Does the actor really need to do all that work? Well, as an actor, aren't you in effect asking, "Is this a picture of a real human being doing real things?" If the answer is yes, the mental track is an essential part of being human, so use it. It is something you can easily do and failing to do it can lead to a lack of believability or authenticity in the actor's work.

In addition, and perhaps more importantly, actual, in-the-moment, dynamic thought pulls the audience into what's happening on stage. But how do we do it? Well, for starters, keep it simple: "Don't speak without an idea in your head." If the actor does it, enough said. On the other hand, if an actor or acting student shows through her work that she is already using thoughts and images in her work, say nothing while you are directing, but then later, in class, you might compliment her on the immediacy of her thoughts and images so that the class is made aware of it. If she does all this intuitively though, be careful not to make her aware of something she does instinctively, and thus kill the very thing she is doing so well.

I have seen actors respond positively to the simple direction, "Don't speak without an idea in your head." That's all they need. But I have also seen actors, even some with considerable experience, not respond to that direction. In that case, here are some ways to go about teaching or learning the technique. This kind of work gets done within the context of using scripted material in monologues or scenes.

The Canadian Stratford Theatre Festival actor, Nicholas Pennell, always said in the workshops he taught, **"The technique is observation."**

> **Exercise:** Begin by observing yourself. Let it be your homework. Watch how your mind moves as you speak. It's fascinating how quickly our minds move and monitor what we say and how pictures are present in our minds as we speak. Or think back on a conversation you had and what your mind did in the process. It's the old "how we do it in life" thing. Notice how, when we quote somebody in a real-life situation, we spontaneously tend to imitate them from the gut. In performance, if the image isn't there, the scripted words can lack vitality and lifelikeness.

Observe others as they speak.

> **Exercise:** In class, have one student give another student the directions to his house. Then have the student

receiving the directions repeat them back. Have the rest of the class observe the student repeating the directions to watch the mental energy. Afterward, ask the student repeating back whether she saw pictures or merely memorized it.

Exercise: Have students tell the class about a personal experience, one that energizes or excites them. It's amazing how often the real-life reading of a line is the very opposite of what you might imagine from the mere reading of the script. One student told of an experience when he was working in the box office and he was held up by a burglar. When he said, "And then he pulled out a gun," he actually laughed, as he related it to his audience.

Exercise: Have students watch good actors on film thinking and seeing images as they speak. Have them watch for the complexity and changes of thought in the actors' eyes. See how these come out of a connection with their partners and how they advance the story. Tell them they may need to go back and watch a film two or three times to really catch this, but it is worth doing. There is an acting lesson right before their very eyes. Our best actors are marvelous at this. Make a CD/DVD of select moments of actors at their best doing inner-monologue work, which you can stop and start to observe and discuss this work.

I've found that Harold Pinter's *Betrayal* provides a good example of this technique vividly at work. The play is about a love triangle in which, in a key scene, the wife must admit to her husband that she is having an affair. They are in Venice. The husband comes back to their hotel room from the post office and he says to his wife that he found a letter from his best friend addressed to her. He carries on wittily, casually making some small jokes about the incompetence of the Venetian post office, and his interaction with them. She comes to realize that he has figured out that she's having an affair, but rather than challenging her with what he suspects, he continues to torture her with his string of carefree, humorous remarks and off-hand comments. Eventually she admits to the affair. On Broadway, in the moment before her confession, there was a pause—a thought-filled pause before she spoke. The actors, Roy Scheider and Blythe Danner, waited for sometimes five seconds, and at one performance 17 seconds before she spoke. Now there is thinking on stage at its best. In the film of *Betrayal*, it is interesting to watch the moment when the wife realizes that *he knows*. And it was not just before she confesses. The actor made the decision to make the realization well before that big moment.

Sonia Moore, in her book *Training an Actor,* has her students write out the inner monologue. She urges them to find and develop thoughts and images that excite and stimulate them, and she goes on at some length to instill this technique. She stresses that it should be fun for the actor to do. Is there a problem to be figured out? A mystery? Is there a discovery to be made? Are there surprises that happen? As one director has said, "Don't report; discover!"

Now let's look at this technique (actual thoughts and images) in the context of scripted work.

Exercise: If real thinking or images are lacking, the teacher can try to stimulate them by adjusting the givens, that is, by working with or against the other actor to force the issue. The teacher or director can stop the scene and whisper to one actor to interrupt the other actor with simple questions, such as, "Why?" "Did she really say that?" Or have one actor visibly show a lack of interest in the other, which can pull her into the reality of the scene. In my experience, this triggers a mental energy that is both real and alive. And it's fun to do and fun to watch. Once the teacher or director starts whispering to one actor, the other one knows something is up and gets on his toes for what might be coming. In my experience, acting students really take to that kind of work and enjoy playing the game.

Here's an **example** of the above technique in action during a rehearsal. I was directing a production of *Eccentricities of a Nightingale* by Tennessee Williams, (his reworking of *Summer and Smoke*) in which the uptight spinster, Alma, is desperately in love with the young doctor, John, but due to her emotional repression, finds it difficult to talk honestly with him. In their first scene together, he sneaks up behind her while she is sitting on a park bench and lights a firecracker, which causes her to jump off her seat. What follows is a scene in which she, in her attempt to connect with him, rattles on in a highly nervous string of conversation that only reveals her anxiety. What was happening in the scene was that the actor was simply rattling, and the sense of idea and mental connection was not there. Only the effect of empty rattling was there. So, I asked the technical director if he had any starting pistols in his props stash, and he said that he had three: a small one, a medium one, and a big loud one. I asked for the loud one, and at rehearsal that night, had Doctor John fire off the starting pistol as a firecracker substitute. Well, the actor really did jump, so we had a sense of what the firecracker effect did to her. But after that, she went back to rattling off *words* rather than *ideas and images*. So, out of her hearing, I asked John, to fire off the gun if he lost interest in what she was saying, if her speech wasn't holding him. Well, once she started to just jabber, he would slowly lift the gun as if he was going to shoot it, and Bingo! The real thoughts and images flew out of her.

Here's an **example** of an image at work from the production of *The Diary of Anne Frank* that I was directing. The characters in the play are hiding from the Nazis and living in fear of being discovered. At one point, Anne has a nightmare and wakes up screaming. The actor playing the role was a good Anne, but in this moment, we needed more of a horrifying, intense scream, so the danger of being discovered was realistically possible. I showed the actor a picture I had found of a Nazi soldier holding a gun to the head of a child. The next day at rehearsal, the actor told me that she'd had a nightmare that night. I said, "Hey, Mary Ann, that is great!" And when the moment came in the run of that scene, she let out a cry that shook the rafters. Very scary. The image did the trick.

Keep in mind that, with all these exercises and techniques, however, there is a danger. With this real-thoughts technique, you must be careful not to get all up in your head. That might sound contradictory since the head is where the thoughts and images reside. But when the actor focuses on the technique rather than the actual communication that is happening between two people, the result can come across as too heady and not authentic. The idea is not to be thinking about thinking but to give yourself completely to the action of the scene. Then you will be fine.

CHAPTER FOUR

TALK *TO* OTHER PEOPLE, NOT *AT* THEM

Communication

Just because you are talking doesn't mean somebody else is listening.

Having thoughts and images in our heads is not a solitary exercise. The thoughts and images now need to be communicated to another person or persons on stage. That's another doable step in the process.

In life, we talk *to* each other, but on stage, in a scene, it is easy to slip into "performing" the language rather than actually communicating. For example, in a rehearsal of *The Misalliance* by George Bernard Shaw, after we ran one of the scenes, I asked the actor playing Tarelton, "Do it again, but this time really ask the question." According to him, a light bulb went on in his head, and he realized what he wasn't doing. We reran the scene, and he did indeed ask the question, and in fact rooted the language and made honest connections with the others in the scene. We didn't need exercises to get what needed to happen. Simply asking for something that we do every day in life solved the problem.

And what is the problem? Well, if someone is up there performing the language, I, the listener, am watching him do just that. I am watching his performance, but I am not getting pulled into the living reality of the scene, which moves the play forward. Observing how actors handle questions on stage is one of the easiest ways of spotting falseness in the work. There is an actual connection we make when we ask a question in real life (unless it's a rhetorical question). We usually watch our question land on the other person, which doesn't mean that we become like a glaring trial lawyer in court, but we are very much aware of the other person's response when we ask that question.

Getting back to Shaw's *The Misalliance*, the son, Johnny, has three speeches, in which he states his reaction to "art," all of which fly in the face of his father, Tarleton, who responds, "You don't cultivate your mind, Johnny. You don't read."

Johnny
Yes, I do. I bet you what you like that, page for page, I read more than you, though I don't talk about it so much. Only, I don't read the same books. I like a book with a plot in it. You like a book with nothing in it but some idea that the chap that writes keeps worrying, like a cat chasing its own tail. I can stand a little of it, just as I can stand watching the cat for two minutes, say, when I've nothing better to do. But a man gets fed up with that sort of thing. The fact is, you look on an author as a sort of god. I look on him as a man that I pay to do a certain thing for me. I pay him to amuse me and to take me out of myself and make me forget.

Tarleton
No. Wrong principle. You want to remember. Read Kipling. "Lest we forget."

And then Johnny follows with two even longer speeches on the same subject that obviously demand an active mental track of ideas that Johnny must not only own but also transfer to Tarleton and the other characters in the room. When I directed this scene, the actor had to get beyond his tendency to perform the language so that he could make the ideas he was communicating real and immediate to his father. As we rehearsed, I found myself saying, "Nick, you had me with the first speech but not the second and third." The next rehearsal it would be, "Nick you nailed one and two, but not number three." In time he nailed them all, but much had to do with his need to communicate, even compete with his father, using the weapons he had in his arsenal, his very own ideas and his need to use them against his father.

Here's another example of this technique in action. In a rehearsal of Steinbeck's *Of Mice and Men*, George, the newly hired laborer on a ranch, and Slim, the foreman, are seated at a table talking. George is telling Slim about his sidekick, Lennie, and giving Slim some background on his friend. But the actors weren't really talking to each other, so they lost my attention and involvement. I pointed this out to them, and they went out in the hall, sat on the floor, and, while other people were walking by them, did the scene just talking to each other. When they came back to do the scene onstage, it was riveting because of the honest connection and the alive communication. And, of course, they were both playing the scene with very solid actions.

Exercise: Sometimes it can be beneficial for two actors to sit down across from each other at a table and just do a scene that way, without the blocking, and simply communicate. It's a simple technique, but it can put the focus on connecting and interacting.

Exercise: Have the student take the lyrics of a song and say them to a partner, seated on the floor or at a table. I recall one girl doing that very effectively and touchingly with the song, "Crazy."

Michael Langham reportedly believed that the soliloquies in Shakespeare were ideas to be communicated to the audience. It is a terrific idea because then they really become an act of communication with a real listener in mind, rather than one of total self-involvement. Thus, Hamlet's "To be, or not to be" speech could be made as a dialogue with the audience, as opposed to a self-absorbed reflection.

Listening

The next basic communication technique is that of listening. It is easy *not* to listen when you know your lines and the other person's lines as well. But your acting partner is dependent upon your alive presence not only as you speak but also as she speaks. So (here we go again) like we do in life. Isn't it interesting how very sensitive we are when the person we are talking to becomes the least bit inattentive or disconnected? We are also sensitive about when a conversation needs to end.

Exercise: Tell the conversation partner of the speaking character to "let your partner know when she loses you by your inattention." It literally forces the speaking character to be more actively aware of her partner.

Exercise: Stop the scene or monologue and adjust the givens. For example, have the listening character visibly dismiss what is coming at him by shaking his head or even saying "No, no." Or have him be deeply pained by what he hears or fight back. Forcing adjustments in the responses of the listening actor will often cause a more honest, intense communication. The teacher's or director's goal here is to make the scene come alive and be compelling.

I read recently that John Wayne believed listening to be the key to good acting. It may sound simple and naïve to even be talking about it here, but listening is obviously a vital component of communication. It's difficult or impossible to really communicate with someone who isn't listening. In that situation, it often becomes necessary for the speaker to give the listener a reason to pay attention if the connection is going to be maintained.

Exercise: Have students observe themselves as they speak and listen to people in their everyday interactions. Simple as that. Have them notice how their minds work on more than one track as they listen, which is why we so often jump right in after or even while another person is talking. We've been listening but doing some thinking of our own at the same time. Or we've been thinking about what we're going to say next instead of really listening to the person talking to us. Or we've been taking a mental vacation from the conversation to think about something else.

As one final **example** of this technique in action, my wife and I went to see Anthony Hopkins in *Equus* on Broadway. As the play began, Hopkins entered, came downstage, and began talking directly to us. And as he got into the speech, he stopped and said "I'm sorry. I'm lost." And for a second or two, I thought he had gone up on his lines. It was that immediate. He had been talking to us. And then, as Martin Dysart, he lost his train of thought.

CHAPTER FIVE

COMING FULLY ALIVE IN THE PRESENCE OF YOUR PARTNER

Making and maintaining an alive, real, dynamic connection with your scene partner(s) is very much a staple of acting, and without that connection, a scene can become merely an exercise in talking *at* each other. Performing is important and will be dealt with later, but for the scene or monologue to come fully alive, the characters need to be in an in-the-moment contact (not necessarily staring at each other but being energized by one another's presence). It is easy to become so self-involved and focused on your own work that you forget the very purpose of the scene is being revealed by the interaction between you and the other actor(s).

All the best actors maintain this vital connection with their other cast members. I watched this early on when I apprenticed at the Cincinnati Summer Playhouse. The effect of it was to draw the audience into the world of the play as they watched "real people doing real things," as George Bernard Shaw called it. My prior example of Luther Adler in *A View from the Bridge* illustrates this quite vividly. His directorial advice was, "Look at me" before we illegals were carted off, and in that moment of looking at him his dynamic connection with us pulled us in.

So, what does this maintaining a lively presence and connection involve, and how do we do it? First let's look at the relationship between characters. Michael Shurtleff, in his book, *Audition,* deals with this technique quite effectively. He minimizes the factual relationship (wife, husband, son, daughter), and asks, "How do you feel about him or her"? Plays are most often about people who make our stomachs turn over when we are in contact with them. So, what is the nature of the emotional pull for this character in this scene?

When we look at the final scene between Peter and Anne in *The Diary of Anne Frank*, the relationship between the characters is obvious because of the prior scenes about them. Initially, Peter is irritated, even maddened, by Anne's playfulness and upbeat energy. As the relationship grows over two years, he comes to admire her spunk and eventually becomes attracted to her. Is it love? Well, perhaps something approaching that, depending on where the actor and director intend to go with it. But he is drawn to her spirit and physicality, and both he and Anne come to prize the time they spend together in his room when they can be alone. They respect each other, and by the last scene have come to depend on each other. And all this is clear in the script itself.

To take this a bit farther, let's look at what Peter feels about some other characters in the play: He respects and admires Mr. Frank, is embarrassed by his parents and their bickering and his mother's flirting with Mr. Frank, and he is so furious about Mr. Dussel that he wants to punch him. Our personal feelings for specific people help define our relationship to them. And it usually shows.

But what about the scenes in which the feeling for the other is not so obvious? What about the characters in any of Chekhov's major plays? Or the Crooks and Lennie relationship in *Of Mice and Men*, which we will look at shortly. It is seductive to examine those kinds of relationships on an analytical level, but how does Crooks actually feel about Lennie? Whatever the feeling is, it must have something to do with the fact that he opens up to Lennie and tells him some personal things. He says that he can tell Lennie anything and Lennie won't even know what the hell he is talking about. Now that may tell us something about what Crooks thinks of Lennie, but what are his feelings toward him? The same question can be asked of Curley's wife. What does she feel about Lennie?

Shurtleff asks about the love in scenes, particularly in scenes where other emotions seem to dominate, such as those between Tom and Amanda in *The Glass Menagerie*. He explores the feeling deeply as he analyzes an acting class scene and steers the exploration beyond the trap of surface judgements, pulling it into a deeper, more important level. I worked with an actor who had a habit of saying, "Oh he (the character) just wants to…" I stopped him and said, "Pete, things in plays are never just anything." If it's not important enough to remain in the scene and you just want to leave, then just do it. End of scene…or cut it.

I recall reading somewhere that when Mike Nichols directed *Uncle Vanya* (a brilliant production), he began by asking the cast to consider how they, the characters, felt about each other. It intrigues me that he would give the cast that direction right off the bat.

So how you feel about the other character is vitally important to you, to the play, to the audience. It keeps you in the space. It magnetizes and vitalizes the connection between you. It may very well be subterranean, but it is there all the same and propels you forward. It gives you a reason for your action. It brings complexity to your work and keeps you from merely making the most obvious judgmental choice in a relationship.

Watch for this sense of being totally alive from actors on stage and especially on film, where the camera reveals it so beautifully. Look at Vanessa Redgrave in *Yanks*, a film with a good cast, but her work is especially radiantly alive.

I realize that "making it come alive" is a large topic and has within it many of the other techniques discussed here and elsewhere, but I have come to believe that when the actor, no matter what level of his development, is expected to make the work a living thing, he becomes engaged in trying to make this happen. It helps guard against slick or mechanical acting.

Opening Up to Your Partner

When I taught at UWSP, I spent a lot of time getting the acting students to open up, that is, to make vital contact with the other actors in their scenes, to have encounters with them and not be afraid to even interfere with them. A starting point was simply to give them the permission to make the connection personal, active, and alive. I found that, in the main, they were quite ready and even eager to try this, and, in the process, come to realize how important it is to the craft.

At the same time, we explored ways to allow the other characters to affect us as well. Being open and vulnerable became a goal of the work. "How can she hurt you?" and questions like that became triggers to deepen the connection between persons. Give the actor playing the other character some power in the scene, no matter the character's status.

In *A Christmas Carol*, two people come to Scrooge's counting house to ask for some money for the poor. Scrooge dismisses them with cold-hearted comments about "decreasing the surplus population" and the like. It would seem on the surface that Scrooge simply turns angrily on them and gets rid of them. Yes, but what if they have some power too, if they cause Scrooge to reflect on himself or threaten to touch a soft spot in him? Subconscious, perhaps, but there all the same. They have some power. Emily and George have tremendous power over each other in the drugstore scene in *Our Town*, not chest-thumping, egomaniacal power but a much deeper, almost all-on-the-line power.

I cautioned students not to fall into the "suit of armor" way of acting, in which you enter a scene totally confident that you know what you are doing, and, "by God, nothing the other person can do will touch me. Hey, I know my lines, so now get out of my way."

So, what are some ways we can go about learning this skill and putting it into practice? Well, first the teacher or director can simply ask for it. Sounds simple, but often enough, just inviting an actor to open-up to a scene partner can do it. Why make it more complex if a simple statement or question will do it. Peter Brook, in his book *The Empty Space,* said that he likes to appeal to the actor's imagination with statements such as, "She's leaving you."

For your homework, pay attention to how this business of connection occurs in your own or others' real-life situations. Look at the dynamic connection between two people who are about to kiss or punch each other. Stage work needs to be at least that compelling. I was walking down Broadway behind a man who was stopped for a few beats by a prostitute who asked him, "Would you like a date?" There was nothing harsh or ugly about it. She didn't look like a tart. She just made a very personal contact without any overt sexual veneer, but it was a marvelous example of a real human connection. Very alive. He said, "No."

And what does that say about the relationship that goes into those moments? For someone who really wants to do some acting, this is actually a fun part of the process, dangerous in its application, but safe in the down-deep awareness that it is a fictional situation and we are protected.

In production or scene work, the teacher or director can once again "adjust the givens" by changing the patterns of the physical (blocking, stage business) or psychological (feelings, emotions) elements. In fact, that becomes an improvisation without changing the dialogue. Simply pulling one actor aside and whispering something to him, immediately puts the other actor on alert that "something's about to change, and I'd better be ready for it."

Exercise: If necessary, certain exercises can invite two actors to open-up to each other, to be available to each other. For example, have two actors sit on the floor cross-legged, facing each other, and tell them to simply make eye contact. Then have them begin to communicate with each other without words, sending out messages such as, "You are terrific," "You are sad," as prompted by cards that you provide to them. This exercise allows the actors to open up to each other and get personal. It gives them permission to connect, and when it works right, it can be fun too.

Exercise: Ask two actors to take the lyrics of a song and say them to each other with feeling. Make it personal. Risk it. Hey, it's what actors do.

Exercise: Have the actors mill around in a circle weaving in and out of the circle but stopping, to shake hands and say "hello" to each person they encounter. Ask them to open up, to make a genuine connection, to make themselves authentically available to one another. Then try it with specific relationships in mind but be careful not to play-act. Keep it honest.

Exercise: Have the actors run their lines across the table from one another. This takes the blocking (stage directions) out of the scene and can prompt the actors to make a more believable connection. Spencer Tracy said, "Look at the other fellow, and tell the truth." Easy to say, more challenging to do. Judi Dench says that "I don't know what I am going to do in a scene until I know what the other actor is going to do."

Exercise: Have students watch how it looks when fine actors make vibrant connections on stage or in film.

Have them look at Annette Bening, for instance, in *20th Century Women*, when she really goes after her scene partner. Have them look in her eyes and imagine playing a scene with her. Ask them, "If she came at you like that, do you think you could hold your own? Sure, you could, and she would help you."

I wonder if "opening up to your partner" isn't, in part, a state of mind for the actor. It begins with a knowledge that it's an essential part of what you do as an actor, and it follows with a readiness to do it.

CHAPTER SIX

WHAT MIGHT IT BE LIKE IF...?

Imagination

At the Tony Awards ceremony some years ago, a certain actor's name was called out as the winner. He made his way to the stage amid great applause, accepted the statue, held it, looked at it and said, "I have this problem with reality." It got a huge laugh, because, of course, he was in a room full of people who knew exactly what he meant, people who made their livings inhabiting imaginary worlds. That's the job. No getting around it. Much of their success depends upon their coming to life in those unreal but real worlds.

A friend of mine was cast in a small part in Shakespeare's *Henry V* with Christopher Plummer as the lead. At the end of one scene, as Henry's men were exiting the king's presence, they were showing him signs of respect by bowing, nodding and stooping, but my friend, in his youthful exuberance, gave the king a high five. Plummer roared: "He's a KING! Not a 'bleeping' basketball player!"

My friend had threatened Plummer's imaginary world. Plummer, in his own book, *In Spite of Myself*, calls himself out on this same point. When he was a young actor, he had a role in *The Lark* with Julie Harris in the lead. Offstage, he mentioned to her that he loved what she did in a certain moment, and she hollered to him: "Shut up! Shut up! Now you've made me conscious of it!" I believe her message was, "You have risked pulling me out of the imaginary world and made me think of my acting."

The great English actor of the latter 19th and early 20th centuries, Ellen Terry, said, "Imagination! Imagination! I put it first years ago, when I was asked what qualities I thought necessary for success on the stage. And I am still of the same opinion. Imagination, industry [hard work] and intelligence...the 'three I's' are all indispensable to the actor, but of these three the greatest is, without a doubt, imagination."

Ellen Terry also said in her autobiography, *Ellen Terry's Memoirs*, that she felt she had success as an actor because she could imagine what it felt like to have her eyes poked out.

Laurette Taylor, the highly respected American actor, who was the original Amanda in *The Glass Menagerie,* said:

> I have been asked to discuss, for the benefit of those who may go on the stage, the qualities which are most important as elements of success. If merely the financial or popular success of a woman is meant, I should say that beauty is more essential than magnetism. But if by success you mean all that is implied by the magical word *art,* I should say most emphatically the reverse. And I should add that imagination is more important than either.

Christopher Plummer, in his book *In Spite of Myself,* has precious little to say about the acting craft, but I get the sense that he is not a big fan of "The Method." At one point, reacting to an actor struggling with the technique of substitution, Plummer said in effect that he thought that the person lacked imagination.

Imagination is the actor's springboard into the role that she is playing in the world of the play. It helps her to believe in the world around her and in the other people in that world. The actor is faced with the challenge of representing an actual person, and behaving credibly, believably in that imaginary role, in that imaginary world. She relies upon her imagination to pull her into it and to keep her there. It is a tool she uses, a technique.

It's all well and good to say that imagination is very important, most important, and that the actor can't do without it, but how do we go about using it, accessing it, letting it affect us?

Let's start by agreeing that we all have imagination. It is important to get beyond the assumption that imagination only exists in the world of the arts, and it is merely an artsy thing to do. Our imagination is often stifled as we mature, e.g., "Stop daydreaming," "Get your head out of the clouds," "Face reality," and so on. The problem is that in many areas of adult life, and in acting especially, we need to use our imagination.

We often use our imagination in life, even though we may not be consciously aware that we're doing so. We engage in fantasies of love, hate, revenge, or sex. We run "what I should have done" scenarios, or "what I'm going to do" scenarios in our heads, all the time. We create "what if" scenarios, such as, "What would it look like if I moved the furniture around this way?" "What if I planted the garden that way?" "What if I adjusted my sales pitch to employ a different technique?" All of these "what ifs" involve the use of our imagination. So, imagination is a useful tool in life.

An actor friend of mine told me that he once had a job in which he had to take the daily earnings to the bank at the end of the day. To make the job interesting, he would imagine that some robbers were following him, ready to steal his loot and perhaps kill him. So, he weaved and dodged through traffic to try to evade them. In his imagination, it all became a great melodrama.

Another very good professional actor told me that when he was playing Petruchio in *The Taming of the Shrew,* he and the actor playing Kate developed an intense physical attraction in the greenroom before the performances, and as the run of the show moved on, the sexual tension between them became greater and greater. There was no touching, no acting it out in real life, no talking about it, but this imagining themselves to be lovers truly affected their work on stage, and it made the tension between Kate and Petruchio compelling.

When I was directing *The Diary of Anne Frank*, as part of my morning walk, I would look at houses and try to imagine which ones might be good for hiding out from Nazis, how I might be able to survive in there if someone would give me sustenance, food and water, and what it might feel like if the Nazis were out in the streets.

And the thing is, these scenes are often fun to do, not unlike children at play.

I found that simply asking the actor or student actor to imagine something is the quickest way to get at it. I also found that most of them want to play, enjoy it, and are ready to jump in and do it. Given the freedom to play, they enjoyed the ride. Why make it more complicated if you don't have to?

Later, if they continue in the work, they can be introduced to some advanced techniques, but I found that to overdo those can paradoxically put up barriers to creativity.

As I have stated before, my preference as a teacher and director is to get to script work quickly, so I find it productive to encourage the use of imagination as soon as we sketch out the action (blocking) and get rid of the scripts.

Here is a potentially useful concept, which if you choose to believe it, might help free the imagination and serve as a springboard into character. When Dick Cavett was doing his evening show many years ago, he interviewed a man who had written a book about a certain tribe in Africa (I think they were called the Eeke.). This tribe had been living on the edge of the desert, which had eventually encroached upon their land and made the growing of crops almost impossible. They were desperate. One night, they were sitting around a fire eating when one of their small children crawled away into the semidarkness. A leopard appeared and moved toward the child. The Eeke all sat and watched while the leopard grabbed the child and ate it. They did nothing. Just sat there. Cavett said, "What a disgusting group of people! Aren't you repulsed?" And the author said, "No, I think we all have the capacity to be many things. These people were starving to death. The child was one less mouth to feed. And I believe that most of us in the same circumstances, might very well behave the same way." When the author did a kindness for one of the older women of the tribe, she began to cry and said she remembered a time when they all behaved that way.

If you can believe that you have the capability to be many kinds of people, then you might very well be able to accept the fact that you could indeed be almost anyone. With the proper training growing up, and being surrounded by a certain group of people, could I become a king? Why not? As I understand it, when Anthony Hopkins played Hitler, he had to enter the Führer's mindset. A friend of mine, whose parents were professional actors in Latvia, told me that his father said to him, "When you grow up, you might become a doctor, a lawyer, a carpenter, a businessman, a teacher, but if you become an actor, you can be all of these things."

A second potentially useful concept is to try not to judge the character. That may sound obvious, but novice actors can be ensnared by this trap. To judge is to stand outside the character, when the real need is to get inside him. There is an oft-told story of Laurence Olivier and Tyrone Guthrie meeting on the streets of London and Guthrie asking Olivier what he was doing. Olivier launched into the fact that he was rehearsing to play Sergius in Shaw's *Arms and the Man* and that he was having a terrible time with it. He went on and on complaining about the character's bad qualities. When he finished, Guthrie said, "Well, if you don't like him, you won't be much good at playing him, will you?"

I like that story because it says a lot about whom you are playing and what you might imagine him to be—from the character's point of view. It would be easy enough for the actor playing Anne Frank to say that, "Oh when I (Anne) was 13, I was a brat." Well, to Peter, and maybe her mother, Anne appeared to be that, but for the reality of having to play the role and for doing the play as written, it might be more useful to say that she was a girl in love with life and even the people in it. Her love permeates every scene she's in, such as the Hanukkah scene, where she manages to give gifts to everybody. She wants to bring joy to others, and she does. She needs to bring some spirit into the world she's inhabiting. The fun of hiding Peter's shoes for example. So, the actor's task is to imagine and tap into that. Why? Because it serves the play. How? She might think back to moments where she (the actor) has felt joy, been the spirted one on occasion, made people laugh, felt positively about a person or people as a springboard to what Anne must be like. She really does believe that people are good at heart.

Sometimes these things come easily for an actor. Simply asking yourself to *go there* is all that is needed. Or the actor can find her own stimulation, or a director or teacher can. It is the willingness to use the imagination that is the key. One professional actor I know talked about the challenges in trying to access some things that he had to try hard to imagine. But, when he was playing the lead in *She Stoops to Conquer*, he said, "Tell me I'm tongue-tied when I am in the presence of a beautiful woman, and I know exactly how to do that!"

Here's another story about an actor using the imagination. The great Italian actor, Eleonora Duse, talked about playing Juliet when she was young and spending much time researching the role. But, she said, "If I had to do it today, I'd go to Verona and imagine." When I tell that story, I recall a photograph of a balcony in Verona that people believe might have been Juliet's balcony. Just that picture can trigger the imagination, as might the photo of the cramped and ugly rooms where Anne Frank's family spent two years, never able to go outside.

Or let's look at the Crooks scene again with this in mind. What might the actor playing Crooks do to imagine and access the intense sense of loneliness it takes to play that role. He might begin with seeing if he can find some moment in his own life where he felt cut off from friends and family, or he might imagine this happening. "What if..." he was suddenly left alone? By himself? On his own? This might come quickly and easily in a flash, or it might help if he uses the circumstances of the play—his being relegated to reading; mending his bad back, which could land him jobless; and recalling the pictures of his past when things were good at his father's place. This and the intense need to connect with someone is at the heart of that role, and the actor relies on his imagination to generate it.

Now, consider how your character sees other characters in the play. Start with how Peter might perceive Anne, from the beginning of the play to the end. Much of that is in the script, as it is in any well-written play. Peter even articulates it in one scene.

> **Exercise:** As a classroom exercise, have the students sit around in a circle and make observations about another actor's character from a play they are working on. Let's take for example characters from *The Diary of Anne Frank*. Peter might look at Anne, who might look at her mother, who might look at Mr. Dussel, who might look at Peter, and so on. Just look at them and imagine prior events in their lives. Have the student actors consider how they actually feel about the character they're looking at and what they think of them too, only without getting pulled into a judgmental point of view. As the teacher, you can guide and stimulate this exercise in imagination by inviting each person to look at her target character as she might in the play. Each person in the circle is an observer and imaginer, as well as a subject of imagination and observation. Of course, each actor can also do this exercise on her own, with the actor playing another character, or with her own mental picture of that other actor in character. The goal here is for the student to begin to see the other actors as the characters they are portraying in the play, as well as to get in touch with how their character feels about

the other characters and thus to stimulate the imagination in ways that are immediately relevant to the script. Remember that you, as teacher or director, can also use your own imagination to devise imagination exercises for yourself.

Work with the imagination is ultimately a matter of personal choices, that is, the actor must find images, thoughts, and details that appeal to him and ring his bell. The sharper the detail, and the more personal it is, the better. And ultimately, the actor wants these images, thoughts, and details to create a feeling or physical response in him. Let them be that strong and appealing. And, again, have fun doing it.

One final thought about all this. In the late 1960's a superb actor, Brewster Mason, played Falstaff for the Royal Shakespeare Company in England. He told us about his process playing Sir John, which he did over the course of a few months. At one point, while he was still performing the role, his wife said to him, "What are you doing?" He asked her what she meant, and she said that he was shouting out a bit and giving her orders, like "Saddle my horse!" and the like. He said he suddenly realized how that character had creeped under his skin without his fully realizing it. He said, "In a month I will give the last performance of him, and I will hate to say goodbye to the old man."

Bringing it Alive

When I was an apprentice in summer stock, a noted director, Peter Kass, was brought in to direct a play at the Cincinnati Summer Playhouse. He had a fascinating directing style. As he worked with actors in rehearsal and wanted to give a direction, he went down on the stage (it was a theatre in the round) and would talk to an actor privately, quietly and then return to his seat in the house. He got real-life work from his actors as a result. Under his direction, the characters became real human beings interacting with each other, and in doing so brought the play totally to life.

At one point in the play, there was to be an off-stage scream by four girls who had just discovered a huge fire. The effect of this was horrifying as their screams pierced the air. One of the screamers told me that Kass spent at least 15 minutes describing this frightful fire to the girls, in such minute detail that they could see the fire in all its terrifying specifics, and they were terrified. He got the result he wanted, and it served the play perfectly. This was not four girls merely hollering off stage. Anybody can do that, but for an actor it is much more. It is ultimately more satisfying and more fun, as it is for the audience too. For me this is a prime example of a director and actors bringing the play totally alive.

This morning I read a review of a new TV series in *The New York Times* in which the reviewer said that the show, "seemed more play-acted than lived-in." And this brings me to a fundamental phase of the acting work that I call bringing it alive.

I realize that this is a large topic that includes many aspects of the acting craft, but I found it important to let my acting students know that in-the-moment vitality is a main goal in the work, and that it is achievable even for novice actors, perhaps not with the complexity and depth of seasoned actors, but to a considerable extent all the same. And in some paradoxical ways, it's all the novice actor knows how to do. Here's an example: When I directed a production of *Our Town*, in the drugstore scene between George and Emily, when they reveal their love for each other and commit to a life together, the scene came totally alive at the first blocking rehearsal. There is no blocking, as such in this scene, because George and Emily are seated at a counter, sipping sodas and talking. It was very moving. My only real concern was whether they could keep the life of it through all the rehearsals, and especially in performance, and they did.

Of course, this bringing it alive doesn't usually happen right off the bat when we begin to work on a scene or play. It takes time to develop, but we know that it's our ultimate goal.

So, what does that really mean, bringing it alive? For me, it means taking the work beyond mere performance, and making it breathe of real life. It means that, for the actor, the events of the imaginary world are things that she believes in, is absorbed by, and has fun doing, like kids do. My granddaughter, age seven, likes to play "waitress." She has a menu of foods, appetizers, main course, vegetables, desserts, and she comes in and takes our orders, then goes back in the other room and makes the meals out of Play-Doh. She does this because it's fun. She believes in it totally. She's not "playing at it." And she even cautions me, "No jokes!" meaning "Don't break the reality of this!" For her, the Play-Doh meals are real; the making of the food is real; the fact that she is a waitress is real.

For the actor, the events of the play are vital happenings he can believe in, as are his relationships to the other people in the play. The place, the weather, all the things that surround him are things that become real for him, so that he can believe in them. Or, he can just perform them. For clarity here, when I use the word "perform," I mean all the technical elements of the work that go into the shaping of a scene, blocking and business, vocal choices, and the like. These are vitally important and usually precede the "bringing it to life," but they are not the final goal of the work. Ian McKellen once said that the first and most basic skill for an actor is to be audible. Tough to argue that. Actors, of necessity, must spend a great deal of time and effort learning techniques and putting them into practice. But the techniques of acting are not ends in themselves. Bringing the play alive is the essential goal.

In my directing work, I like to start blocking the play at the outset, unless the density or the stylistic demands of the script necessitate some table work first. I allow roughly a third of rehearsals for blocking, retrace, and line learning, and then get into the fun part, which is trying to make it come to life. I know there are many ways to bring the work to life, but I found this approach worked best for me.

CHAPTER SEVEN

WHAT AM I FEELING?

Emotion

"Oh, what a rogue and peasant slave am I!
Is it not monstrous that this player here,
But in a fiction, a dream of passion,
Could force his soul to his own conceit
That from her working all his visage wann'd
Tears in his eyes, distraction in his aspect,
A broken voice, and his whole function suiting
With forms to his conceit? And all for nothing,
For Hecuba!
What's Hecuba to him, or he to Hecuba
That he should weep of her?"

This is Hamlet's reaction to one of the travelling actors who enacted a speech about the death of Hecuba and broke down in tears in the process.

When Kevin Spacey received an Oscar, someone said to an actor friend, "He gave the same speech at the Screen Actors Guild awards and broke down at the same spot," to which an actor friend replied, "Yes, they call it acting."

Last night I watched the Golden Globe Awards give a lifetime achievement award to Meryl Streep. When the camera swept across the large room as Streep stood before them, the intense admiration of her was palpable. Here she was, addressing a large gathering of her peers, whose respect for her was intense. It was inspiring to see a group of people who worked in the same profession, who knew what it takes to do it well, vigorously applauding someone who was literally at the top of her profession. Here was an actor who could portray Florence Foster Jenkins and let us see the complex inner workings of that person.

Actors live in an imaginary world in which they must believe, so that we, the audience, might believe and be drawn in. In order to do that, they are, for the most part, bound by necessity to experience the thoughts and feelings of the characters they inhabit. To do this well, they bring their very souls to the performance to achieve the effect they desire. They put themselves through 2½ hours of an emotional wringer every night on stage, which is certainly the equivalent of any job or life situation that requires an immense amount of physical and emotional effort.

Now I know that there are some naysayers who disagree on this issue of an actor's need to actually experience the thoughts and emotions of a character. But I'd like to believe that most actors do indeed feel the need to go there emotionally, and I return to my "Saint Paul moment" being onstage with Luther Adler, who brought a magnetic emotional energy to his work every night. His pre-show preparation included walking the track, in costume, with his bag of candy that he had bought for his niece before he came home from work.

Now can you fake this? One actor said with an ironic twist, "Can you fake sincerity?" Or as another actor said of Spencer Tracy, "He looks at you and tells you the truth, and if you can fake that, you've got it made."

Certainly, performances need to be shaped, but this shaping can be a substitute for the real thing when it comes to the emotional demands of a script. Here's a case in point: In a performance of *The Royal Family*, the actor Jan Maxwell played the female lead. In a play that demanded flamboyant acting (the Barrymore family was the inspiration for the characters), Maxwell consistently played with a great flair as well as keeping the character honest, rooted, and real. I was seated in the second row, and at the end, when her mother dies in a chair down center, Maxwell knelt to embrace her dead mother, and a tear rolled down her cheek. Because of the physical shaping of that moment, and because of the very size of the theatre (Broadway) she could certainly get away with not going there emotionally, certainly not to the extent of real tears. She could have hidden her face in her mother's neck. But she didn't settle for that. And what she did was completely consistent with the reality of the moment in the character's life.

I've had a few other experiences of watching an actor up close when, because of my close proximity to the stage, I could see directly into the actor's eyes. At the Shaw Theatre Festival, the actor Peter Millard was playing a role in Shaw's *Widowers' Houses* in which he had to unload his fury and anguish on another character, and it all just gushed out of him. Not a moment of slickness, only the real thing. Same with the actor playing Nurse Ratched off-Broadway. Up close we could see the rage and fear in her eyes. Or Jessica Tandy in *The Proposition* breaking down at a climactic point. If it was faked, then it was true magic. Examples of this kind of thing abound on stage, and especially in film these days.

All of this is not to suggest that anger and crying are the only two emotions that an actor need display. The entire panoply of feelings that are the stuff of being human are at the core of dramatic performance. Embarrassment, sexual hunger, despair, vulnerability, uncontrollable laughter, the list goes on and on. It was such fun watching Emma Stone and Ryan Gosling in the film *La La Land* experiencing the sheer joy of being in one another's presence when that relationship was at its most positive moments. Or watch the confusion in Emma's eyes as she experiences the pain and then tries to conceal it, when she learns that they might be separated for a couple of years to pursue their careers. The sheer complexity of the thoughts and emotions that run through her being, and serve the scene beautifully, are a joy to watch. And then there is the intense vulnerability that is at the basis of all this, plus her need to conceal her real feelings from him, as we often do in life, adding to the complexity and real-life quality of it all.

So how does an actor get the emotional response that she needs at the exact moment that she needs it, especially the big moments? Are there techniques for making this happen? She knows from the script that she must deal with some complex thoughts and hit some emotional highs in certain scenes. How might she go about it?

There are many systems of acting and acting exercises that attempt to address this challenge. Ideally, the events of the script, who the character is, and the actor's own sensibilities, bring her to the emotional state she wants to create. But what if this fails to happen? One of the techniques that came out of The Method System to deal with this challenge is "substitution," whereby the actor, as he hits the moment of strong emotional need, substitutes a moment from his past that made a strong impact on him and thinks of it in the moment in the script when he needs it. The famous actor John Gielgud, when asked how he dealt with a major emotional breakdown, said that he thought of his mother in her casket, and he cried. Jose Ferrer imagined the deaths of members of his family, and he said that he killed off everybody one-by-one until he was now down to the dog.

Now there are those who decry this technique on the grounds that it pulls the actor out of the play to achieve the effect. This approach relies on the actor's imagination to do the work of creating the necessary stimuli to pull the actor emotionally into the imaginary world. It stresses the need to vitalize and personalize the world of the play, its events, relationships, and sensory surroundings, in such compelling ways that the needed emotional response is triggered.

In my experience as a director and as a teacher, I found it best not to deal with the emotional side of acting right away when working on a scene for class or in production. Emotion is a by-product of something else, much like sweating is a by-product of running, so my focus was on the "something else" part of the work first. Sketching out the physical actions (blocking, business); the selection of interior actions (intentions...what am I doing?), and work on developing relationships to the other characters (connections with them) can all begin to free up the actor. Emotions can come later, although sometimes, like so many other paradoxical things in acting, they can even come early on in the work.

For example, in the last scene in *Of Mice and Men*, George has to kill his best friend, Lennie. He has Lennie kneel down to look at something far off, puts a gun to his head and pulls the trigger. At the first blocking rehearsal, we set the business, and when we were finished, I noticed a tear running down the cheek of the actor playing George. I said, when no one else was listening, "Thanks for going there, Pete." Did he have to go there? No, because the gunshot happened in a blackout. But sometimes, with a well-written play and a sensitive actor, things like this can happen easily and surprisingly early.

Marlon Brando, when praised for his signature "I coulda been a contender" scene in *On the Waterfront*, said that it was the writing that made it happen. "Anyone, given that material, could have done that scene well," he said. Okay, maybe he was just being modest, but it is a point well taken. A good script alone can grab the actor and free him up to release the emotion.

In *My Fair Lady*, Henry Higgins is desperately trying to get Eliza Doolittle to speak correct English rather than her native Cockney speech. In a series of mini scenes, he works tirelessly, browbeating her to get her to say, "The rain in Spain stays mainly in the plain" correctly. He tries many ways to get her to do it, and when she finally does, there is an explosion of joy from him and his friend Colonel Pickering, propelling them into the song, "The Rain in Spain." The climax and its build-up are so brilliantly written, as is the song, that it's almost impossible not to be caught up in the excitement of it all.

Beyond a good script, what other ways are there to help the actor toward the feeling world of the character? For one thing, let her have her space for a while, as the technical demands of blocking and lines are dealt with. And give her the freedom to find her way with things. Maybe you (the director, teacher) will never have to talk about emotions. She will probably be searching to find them on her own.

But essentially, the most important technique for connecting with the emotional world of the character is the imagination. It's back to Ellen Terry's dictum, "I'm a successful actor because I know what it feels like to have my eyes poked out." So, coach the actor along these lines: Imagine the relationship to your partner. How do you feel about him? Transform him into the person he is to you in the play. What stimulates you about him? Make this a personal thing. Fall in love with him if you need to. What physical traits of his affect you in a particular way? Imagine him as your lover if that's what the play calls for. Let your imagination work for you to create the whole world of the play—the physical things, the feeling things, the events that affect you. Let your imagination go on these things. Fantasize on it all. Create real feeling connections with the other people of the play. Imagine the prior events and the like.

Give yourself the freedom to do these things. Daydream about them. What is sometimes not okay to do in life, for example to daydream, is what you *want* to do as an actor to get where you want to be. If you create physical sensations through your imagination, so much the better. And sometimes what triggers the imaginary leap can happen in a flash. Other times it may take some doing. But release it. Put it to work for you. Make that world of the play leap alive for you. You can do it, if you give yourself the freedom to do it.

Now, is it a law that an actor must experience an emotional response every time she performs? This question has been argued and discussed for a long time, perhaps forever as far as we know, and for some very good reasons. Emotions are elusive things. One day is very different from the next, and we cannot assume that today will feel exactly like yesterday. Actors at the top of their game have been known to talk about how their performance today seemed lacking for them in terms of their inner connections to the world of the play. It's why the shaping of a performance becomes important on those nights when the spirit may be lacking. The physical line, the vocal line, even the internal techniques such as action, inner monologues and the like can free an actor to get through a performance when the experience of true emotions is wanting. A noted actor told me about receiving a "Dear Jane" letter just before a performance, and the only thing she said she could do was to just go with it and use the emotion that she got from that experience.

I think it is a fair generalization that most actors, especially those at the top of their game, are unsatisfied with a mere "technical performance," but some actors really don't want to "go there." I had one actor, in a community theatre production, say to me, "You want me to spill my guts, but I'm not sure I want to do that." (Actually, I wasn't asking him to spill his guts at all). Another very bright young actor, who was playing Sidney Carton in *A Tale of Two Cities,* knowing he had to hit an emotional high spot at one point, said, "I don't know if I can go there," and what leapt out of my mouth was, "But Erik, that's what actors do," and he indeed got there.

There is a story about Jack Nicholson during the filming of *Five Easy Pieces* in which the director asked him to "break down crying" in one scene. Nicholson resisted, but the director kept pushing, and finally Jack said, "Ok, I'll give you one take and that is all!" He did and it's in the film. But those things are risky for an actor, because it is so easy not to be totally credible or vulnerable, and, in his own eyes at least, to look phony. One of the most difficult scenes I ever did was in the world premiere of Lawrence and Lee's *The Night Thoreau Spent in Jail.* In the play, Thoreau and his brother John had to fall down laughing uncontrollably at an incident in Thoreau's relationship with a girlfriend. I never felt that I ever really got there, try as I might. And it was why I marveled so much watching Judi Dench in the TV comedy series, *As Time Goes By.* Among the many things she did so well in that show, she could laugh genuinely when it was called for. No "stage-laugh" there. Always and every time the real thing was there. And if you were faking it, Judi, please never tell me.

So, what are some techniques, some exercises for an actor to use to help access emotion in her work? For starters, the key to much of it is in the imagination, so the exercises mentioned earlier can be very useful here. They are ways to vitalize and personalize the world of the play for the actor. Imagining the reality of the relationships can pull the actor into that world. In *The Diary of Anne Frank*, it might be an energizing choice for Anne to imagine what a future life with Peter might be like. In some ways, he is her world. Take that final thing she says before the Nazis crash in, "Look at us...going on at each other like stupid grownups." Is that a discovery of the moment? Has she even imagined herself as his wife until now? It's only one possibility, but it's the personal part of the acting process. If such an imagined thing works for a particular actor, vitalizes and deepens the relationship with Peter, and creates a "feeling response" of whatever kind, it only serves as an avenue into that emotional world for her.

Finally, and most importantly, the job of emotional release is often important and necessary to tell the story of the play. A case in point: In the early 1980s, the Canadian Stratford Theatre Festival produced a landmark version of *Romeo and Juliet*, in which the gifted actor Max Helpmann played Prince Escalus. The prince is the head of state who appears three times in the play. His first scene comes early on when he breaks up a vicious fight between the young men of the Montague and Capulet families, who have been going at each other with their swords. When Max played the role, he was furious! He raged against them, calling them beasts, threatening them with torture if they didn't put down their swords, while referring to himself as "move-ed." He threatened them that if they ever fought again, he would have them killed. Helpmann's rage was full out, specifically directed (no generalized anger there) as he told the heads of each warring household that he wanted to see each of them privately that day. His fury was scary.

Later in the play, Escalus enters just after Romeo has killed Tybalt. Once again, the prince's anger was monumental as he banished Romeo from Verona and told the kid that if he ever returned to Verona, he would be killed.

The prince's final scene is in the tomb just after some members of both households have discovered the dead bodies of both Romeo and Juliet, and it falls to the priest, Friar Lawrence, to tell the prince what has happened to cause these deaths. A friend of mine, in seeing a different production of the play, expressed her impatience with the friar's going on about something we already know, that is, the prior events of the play which caused this. But when Max Helpmann was Escalus, the need to tell him was clearly necessary, because the demanding, powerful, and angry prince had to be told the whole story. It was dramatically necessary, not unlike a contemporary cop show, where the chief of the crime bureau has to be told what was going on and what actually happened.

I describe this performance at some length because of how necessary the display of emotion can be to drive the story of the play. I've seen a number of productions of this play, but Helpmann's performance of that role stands out for me as the ultimate rendering of who Prince Escalus is, and it is the playwright's intention for this to be so, since he has the character say he is "move-ed."

Another example of emotional depth is the need for the actors to display sexual hunger when the play demands it. In the play, *Abelard and Heloise*, those medieval religious figures, a priest and a nun, fall madly and hungrily in love. In a series of three short scenes, the playwright has the characters reveal their developing and intense physical relationship, which they eventually gratify, and which is at the very core of the story as it evolves. Their deep physical drives are also at war with their needs not to gratify those drives because of their commitments to their vocations. In one of the scenes, Abelard has one of his young followers whip him to drive out his strong sexual needs. So now, the roles as written demand competing emotional drives—a need for complexity in the actors' work. It is surprising how difficult it can be for some actors to generate a real sexual hunger within a fictional situation, particularly when the script demands it, or when the actors are young or relatively sexually inexperienced.

Can emotions be faked? Well, they will certainly need to be shaped physically, but in most cases the actors will want to "go there" to make the scenes and the play work.

In *La La Land*, Emma Stone, as an aspiring actor, goes to an audition for a movie where she must angrily assault another character. She reads one sentence, and the casting director says, "Thank you," and that's the end of her audition. While most actors can identify with this experience, and even laugh about its familiarity (the old "thank you" after just one line), the scene is also very revealing. Ms. Stone simply generalizes the emotion (anger), no depth, no complexity, not at all false, full of energy, but not good enough. It was an object lesson from an actor, who in her own work, is anything but general.

In the film about the revival of *A Chorus Line* for Broadway, we can watch the casting directors look at various actors' auditions for certain roles in that show. One memorable audition is for the character of Paul, a gay young dancer who tells a story about his parents discovering his sexual orientation when they see him on stage in a performance. The auditors watch a few actors read Paul's story, and they are all good, competent actors with strong performance senses. But then a young man takes the script and simply inhabits the role, honestly, personally, with a contained sense of the dynamic and personal pain of it all. He finishes, and the casting director whispers to his team, "Sign him up." Totally honest, totally engaging, not merely performance, but real life happening in front of us.

Richard Gustin in
How to Succeed in Business
University of Wisconsin-Stevens Point

Kathy Kinney
Anything Goes
University of Wisconsin-Stevens Point

Servant of Two Masters, University of Wisconsin-Stevens Point

Mary Ann Ference, Duane Domutz in
The Diary of Anne Frank
Hilberry Theatre
Wayne State University

Kim Cook, Richard Budzinski in
Eccentricities of a Nightingale
Bonstelle Theatre
Wayne State University

Katie Sikorski, Mark Corkins in ***Our Town,*** Hilberry Theatre
Wayne State University

PART TWO
EXTERNAL TECHNIQUES

CHAPTER EIGHT

LOOK AND SEE; LISTEN AND HEAR

Observation

On several occasions, while watching a student production, my wife, Jan, has said to me "I know how this is supposed to sound, but they aren't doing it." I translate that message to mean, "When we speak (in life), we use inflection patterns to convey our meanings." It is a hallmark of our use of language, but to violate it means it is not at all like life, and makes the communication part of the theatre difficult, if not impossible. That's not how we talk, if we want to be understood. And in life we do it all spontaneously, from the gut; we color our speech for clarity.

A strange thing can happen when a person comes to acting. In an attempt to "be dramatic," he can suddenly do things on stage that he would never do in life, such as placing faulty emphasis on a vocal line, making the work untrue as well as incomprehensible. A friend of mine once said, "I don't go to the theatre to process what's going on onstage. I expect the actors to make it clear."

The same thing can happen with physical choices. The Stratford and Shaw theatres actor, Barry McGregor, reacting to the performance of a student actor, responded with, "What human being walks like that?"

I was walking down the street in Cincinnati with a Playhouse actor, Mark Weston, when he spotted a man walking ahead of us. "Look at how that guy walks! Let's follow him." And we did for a few blocks trying to duplicate his walk. Or, as we sat in a bar watching a film on TV, and as Fredrick March entered a scene, Mark said "Look at that...how he comes in...he's never been there before!"

This brings us to the technique of observation, or, looking and listening to life as a means of understanding how we humans do things. But it's easy to violate this once you step on stage. Shakespeare said it best in Hamlet's advice to the players:

> "O, there be players I have seen play--and heard others praise...that, neither having the accent of Christians nor the gait of Christian, pagan, nor man, have so strutted and bellow'd that I have thought some of Nature's journeymen had made men, and not made them well, they imitated humanity so abominably."

When the stalwart Stratford (Canadian) actor, Nick Pennell, taught his acting workshops, he said that "the technique is observation," suggesting that the mainstay of the actor's work is observing.

Watch yourself: how you take an action, use your imagination, how you calculate, how you are affected by a thing of beauty, how you experience pain and the physical result of it, on and on. Get in the habit of doing this. It really is part of your homework, which, for an actor, is ongoing. Make a journal of it if you'd like.

For the actor, the world is her workshop. Looking and seeing things she might use sometime in her work, she builds up a storehouse of images that she can draw upon whenever she needs them. There is a story about the Irish actor, Michael MacLiammoir looking at himself in the mirror to see what total, abject grief looked like as a classic example of self-observation. He almost certainly thought, "I may have the need to use that sometime."

Watch others: how they walk, talk, communicate, manifest internal thoughts and feelings, how they are affected by others, how they eat, laugh, and so on. Look and see. It can be fun.

Watching good actors work is also an important part of observation, not to copy or imitate them but, as Judi Dench has said of observing actors, "You can learn a lot by watching." The first Broadway show I saw was *Fanny* with Ezio Pinza. He had the magnificent voice, of course, but what I remember most vividly is how much at ease he was on stage, at ease in a powerfully commanding way. I also observed how Judith Anderson used the rhythm of language in a melodrama, and the inner monologue of Amy Adams in the film *June Bug* and other films in which she appeared.

I suggest embracing the *joy* of observation. It's fun to do, as well as being very useful for the actor. As I said above, start with yourself.

I believe that observation is a fundamental technique in an actor's toolbox. When Harrison Ford did a film in which he was a trial lawyer, he spent a week going to court to see how the real people did it. Jonathan Winters used to take each day in a week and observe different types of people and animals. He would do birds one day, children the next, four-footed animals on another day, on and on.

Lest we think that observation is only the bailiwick of modern actors, it's instructive to hear that the English acting star, David Garrick (1717-1779) used this technique when he was playing *King Lear*. He visited London's Bethlehem Hospital (Bedlam) and observed an acquaintance of his who had gone mad after having accidentally killed his baby child by dropping him from a third-story window. Garrick said, "It was there that I learned to imitate madness; I copied nature, and to that I owed my success in *King Lear*." That's a lesson in avoiding the general and embracing the specific.

George Abbott, in his autobiography, *Mister Abbott*, tells a story about his directing a show that premiered at a major university, starred Henry Fonda, and used some of the theatre students in support roles. The show rehearsed at the same time as the World Series, and Abbott was bothered by the fact that most of the student actors stayed in the greenroom watching the Series games on TV rather than watching rehearsals. He said that "they could have learned more by watching Hank Fonda go about his work than in a whole year of acting classes."

Look at what Philip Seymour Hoffman did in the film *Capote* and imagine what he must have done in preparation for that role. He didn't do an exact copy of Capote, but he was very specific about his physical, vocal, and internal choices. (And though he didn't look exactly like Truman Capote, he did look almost exactly like a colleague of mine, whom he could not have known.)

Here's another example of my own of the use of observation. I was rehearsing *My Fair Lady*, playing Higgins at Ohio State, and felt stumped a few times as to how to understand the character at a particular moment. I decided that Higgins had something in common with John Morrow, my advisor, so whenever I got stumped, I did what I thought Morrow would do. After the run was over, a colleague of mine, who was a crackerjack actor and acting teacher, said to me, "You were doing John Morrow up there weren't you?" Oops. I got caught. But as he was the only one to comment on it, I felt okay with it.

How might we apply this technique in the classroom or in production? For the classroom, observing each other in class can be useful. Or a monologue incorporating the traits of an observed character can be a way of exploring this technique. Go out in life, find someone that takes your fancy, and see if you can use some of his or her traits in the scripted material.

The trap in this business of observation is to copy or merely imitate something or someone. There is a story about John Gielgud when he was teaching a class. After one of the classes, a group of students were imitating Sir John, who happened upon them doing this. His comment: "In the main, people who are good imitators are not very good actors."

Like all these techniques, it should never become an end in itself. It's a tool. Use it when you need it, but perhaps only then. Think of it this way: If the actor playing Peter in *The Diary of Anne Frank* comes to the role and feels that he knows exactly who this person is, understands him totally, and can find Peter within himself, leave well enough alone. But, if he finds that he has trouble accessing Peter's shyness, or anger, or the love he might feel for Anne, he might want to try observation of himself or others. And when he is finished with the run, he might want to see what choices other actors have made on film or on stage. But never while he is preparing the role or during the run.

To sum up: Grandpa's sense of humor, Aunt Lizzie's great reserve, Aunt Charlotte's upper-class speech, Mom's sense of the absurd, Doctor Bowen's folksy demeanor, Sergeant Hampton's swagger, Dan's monotonic speech, Buck's explosive nature, Pat's developing of an idea, Ed's impulsiveness, Jerry's sense of awe, Otto's sly grin, Phil's bombast, Betty's southern speech, Tony's arch attitude, Barbara's enthusiasm; all these and tons more are fun to observe, and can be useful.

CHAPTER NINE

WHAT HAPPENS IN THIS SCENE?

Tell the Story

Michael Curtiz, the director of *Casablanca*, said of Ingrid Bergman, "She has a good sense of story." I had never heard it expressed quite that way, but it makes great sense. Oh, of course, the director has the responsibility of knowing what the play is about, and he will steer the entire play by the way he answers that question. But the actor should also have a sense of how a story moves ahead, what important points are to be made, and what occurs in the scene to accomplish this. Diane Paulus, the artistic director of The American Repertory Theatre in Boston, reported that when Mike Nichols taught acting, he would watch a scene and then ask the actors, "What happens in this scene?" Or, "Tell me the story of it." That sounds rather basic, and obvious, but it's something that an actor, facing the initial challenges of interior analysis, lines, blocking, and performance concerns, can easily overlook. So, the actor needs the skill to be able to read the play from a story point of view and then see how it moves ahead. Here are some questions for the actor to ask herself about this:

- What happens in this scene?
- What has changed from the beginning of the scene to the end?
- What discoveries do you make in this scene?
- How do the discoveries change you?
- How, technically, might you portray these changes?

Take any scene from a play and try to apply these questions. Look at the Anne and Peter scene for example: Tensions have run high among the people in hiding, since their lifeline, Meip, hasn't appeared in three days. After watching a bitter quarrel between his parents, Peter goes quickly to his room. Seeing his despair, Anne goes to his room to try to calm his fears.

The first thing she does is to tell him how she copes with negative feelings. "I think myself out of it, on a walk in the park," and so on. Peter isn't moved. Then she makes it more personal. "I wish you had a religion, Peter." He says, "No thanks. Not for me." She takes it to an even more personal level. "When I think of the dearness of you, Peter, ... of all these good things, I'm not afraid anymore." Peter says that he just gets mad, but he weakens a bit "...waiting for them to come and get us. And all for what?" She argues that they aren't the only ones who've had to suffer. He says that doesn't make him feel any better. And then she tells him something even more personal, that she knows it is hard to have any faith, "but you know what I sometimes think? I think the world may be going through a phase, the way I was with Mother. It'll pass, maybe not for hundreds of years, but some day. I still believe, in spite of everything, that people are really good at heart." Peter still resists, but not strongly. "I want to see something now. Not in a hundred years." And she says, "But, Peter, if you'd only look at it as part of a great pattern...that we're just a little minute in life...Listen to us, going on at each other like a couple of stupid grownups!" And then she holds out her hand to him. He takes it, embraces her, and they both look up at the sky.

Notice the major change from the beginning moments to the end of this scene. And look at the progression, how the playwright makes the scene move ahead step-by-step. And see how Anne uses an increasingly personal connection as she moves toward her goal. That's what happens in that scene.

I believe this scene is a good illustration of how the actors and the director are very much a part of the playwriting process.

If you look at the stage directions of the original production, you can see how the director (and actors?) have reinforced the playwright's basic progression with the physical choices made by the two actors: moving closer, a slight touch perhaps, pulling away, and reconnecting. The same goes for the emotional connection between them.

Now, let's look at a scene that is not quite so obvious, the Crooks/Lennie scene from *Of Mice and Men* by John Steinbeck to see how this might work. In the play, George and Lennie find work on a ranch in California during the Depression. Lennie, a large man who literally doesn't know his own strength, is slow-witted as the result of being kicked in the head by a mule. George has taken it on himself to be Lennie's caretaker as well as his friend and companion. One Saturday evening, George goes off with some of the other ranch hands to town, but before he does, he cautions Lennie, who is dangerous when he's left on his own, to stay in the bunkhouse until he (George) returns. But Lennie wanders off and, seeing a light in a lean-to room next to the barn, goes to it. This room is the hovel of Crooks, who, because he is Black, is required to live by himself near the barn. Here is the scene between these two men.

(Crooks is seated on his bed in his room. Lennie appears in the doorway)

Crooks
You got no right to come in my room. This here's my room. Nobody got any right in here but me.

Lennie
I ain't doin' nothing. Just come in the barn to have a look at my pup, and I seen your light.

Crooks
Well, I got right to have a light. You go on and get out of my room. I ain't wanted in the bunkhouse and you ain't wanted in my room.

Lennie
Why ain't you wanted?

Crooks
Because I'm black. They play cards in there. But I can't play because I'm black. They say I stink. Well, I tell you all of you stink to me.

Lennie
Everybody went into town. Slim and George and everybody. George says I got to stay here and not get into no trouble. I seen your light.

Crooks
Well, what do you want?

Lennie
Nothing…I seen your light. I thought I could jus' come in and set.

Crooks
I don't know what you're doin' in the barn anyway. You ain't no skinner. There's no call for a bucker to come into the barn at all. You've got nothing to do with horses and mules.

Lennie
The pup. I come to see my pup.

Crooks
Well, God damn it, go and see your pup then. Don't go no place where you ain't wanted.

Lennie
I looked at him a little. Slim says I ain't to pet him very much.

Crooks
Well, you been taking him out of the nest all the time. I wonder the old lady don't move him someplace else.

Lennie
Oh, she don't care. She lets me.

Crooks
Come on in an set awhile. Long as you won't get out an leave me alone, you might as well set down.... All the boys gone into town, hun?

Lennie
All but old Candy. He jus' sets in the bunkhouse sharpening his pencils. And sharpening and figurin'.

Crooks
Figurin? What's Candy figurin' about?

Lennie
Bout the land. Bout the little place.

Crooks
You're nuts. You're crazy as a wedge. What land you talkin' about?

Lennie
The land we're gonna get. And a little house and pigeons.

Crooks
Just nuts. I don't blame the guy you're traveling with for keeping you out of sight.

Lennie
It ain't no lie. We're gonna do it. Gonna get a little place and live on the fat of the land.

Crooks
Set down on that nail keg.

Lennie
You think it's a lie. Bit it ain't no lie. Ever' word's the truth. You can ask George.

Crooks
You travel with George, don't you?

Lennie
Sure, me and him goes ever' place together.

Crooks
Sometimes he talks and you don't know what the hell he's talkin' about. Ain't that so?... Ain't that so?

Lennie
Yeah. Sometimes.

                    Crooks
Just talks on. And you don't know what the hell it's all about.

                    Lennie
How long do you think it'll be before them pups will be old enough to pet?

                    Crooks
A guy can talk to you and be sure you won't go blabbing. A couple of weeks and them pups will be all right. George knows what he's about. Just talks and you don't understand nothing. Well this is just a nigger talkin', and a busted-backed nigger. It don't make no difference if he don't hear or understand. The thing is they're just talkin'. George can tell you screwy things and it don't matter. It's just talkin'. It's just being with another guy, that's all. S'pose George don't come back no more? S'pose he took a powder and just ain't comin' back. What you do then?

                    Lennie
What? What?

                    Crooks
I said s'pose George went into town tonight and you never heard of him no more. Just s'pose that.

                    Lennie
He won't do it. George wouldn't do nothing like that. I been with George a long time. He'll come back tonight…Don't you think he will?

Crooks
Nobody can tell what a guy will do. Let's say he wants to come back and can't. S'pose he gets killed or hurt so he can't come back.

Lennie
I don't know. Say, what you doin' anyway? It ain't true. George ain't got hurt.

Crooks
Want me to tell you what'll happen? They'll take you to the booby hatch. They'll tie you up with a collar like a dog. Then you'll be jus' like me. Livin' in a kennel.

Lennie
(Walking over to Crooks)
Who hurt George?

Crooks
(Recoiling in fear)
I was just supposin'. George ain't hurt. He's all right. He'll be back all right.

Lennie
(Standing over him)
What you supposin' for? Ain't nobody goin' to hurt George.

Crooks
Now set down. George ain't hurt. Go on now, set down.

Lennie
Ain't nobody gonna talk no hurt to George.

Crooks
Maybe you can see now. You got George. You know he's comin' back. S'pose you couldn't go in the bunkhouse and play rummy, cause you was black. How would you like that? Books ain't no good. A guy needs somebody…to be near him. A guy goes nuts if he ain't got nobody. Don't make no difference who it is as long as he's with you. I tell you a guy gets too lonely, he gets sick.

Lennie
George gonna come back. Maybe George come back already. Maybe I better go see.

Crooks
I didn't mean to scare you. He'll come back I was talkin' about myself.

Lennie
George won't go away and leave me. I know he won't do that.

Crooks
I remember when I was a little kid on my ole man's ranch. Had two brothers. They was always near me, always there. Used to sleep right in the same room. Right in the same bed, all three. Had a strawberry patch. Had an alfalfa patch. Used to turn the chickens out in the alfalfa patch on a sunny morning. Me and my brothers would set on the fence and watch 'em…white chickens they was.

                    Lennie
George says we're gonna have alfalfa.

                    Crooks
You're nuts.

                    Lennie
We are too gonna get it. You ask George.

                    Crooks
You're nuts. I seen hundreds of men come by on the road and on the ranches, bindles on their back and that same damn thing in their head. Hundreds of 'em. They come and they quit and they go on. And every damn one of 'em is got a little piece of land in his head. And never a goddamn one of 'em gets it. Jus' like heaven. Everybody wants a little piece of land. Nobody never gets to heaven. And nobody gets no land.

                    Lennie
We are too.

                    Crooks
It's jest in your head. Guys all the time talkin' about it, but it's jest in your head.

    Before we examine how the scene progresses, we need to look at Crooks's action in it. **What is he doing?** Well, Steinbeck has the character boldly state what it is. It's the need to make a connection with someone. He is desperate to make a connection so he "doesn't go crazy" as he says, and he is willing to let that person be Lennie, whom he knows doesn't understand what he is talking about.

When I directed this play, it seemed to me that it was very much about loneliness. Each scene in the play reinforces that idea, especially the climax, where George is forced to kill his one and only friend. Lennie needs George, but George also needs Lennie. Curley's wife needs someone to talk to and talks to Lennie. Slim needs someone like George to talk to, and vice versa. Candy needs the companionship of his old dog. Steinbeck has created a world in which the people are isolated in many ways.

In our production, I told the fine actor playing Crooks that this was not a scene about an angry black man. Yes, there is justifiable anger in it, but it was a scene about an isolated man needing to connect with someone, anyone. The actor said, "I know what you mean." It's what Steinbeck means. It's all right there in the script.

Now let's see what happens in the scene and how it progresses. It begins with Crooks telling Lennie to get out of there, to his (Crooks's) inviting him to sit down as he eventually tells him some personal things. What causes the changes along the way to cause Crooks to invite Lennie to sit down? What does Crooks see in Lennie to allow this change? He sees Lennie's sensitivity to the dog. He sees his naiveté. He tests him about not blabbing about what he has heard. He prods him to respond actively when he suggests that George might not return. He feels comfortable enough to tell Lennie about his past. Each one of these things is a change, a step forward. Progression. It's what happens in the scene. I believe that an actor needs to be able to see this and to use it. And, of course, an actor might make different choices about the moment-to-moment elements of the scene, especially depending on what his partner does. But no matter what, he must account for how the changes happen from start to finish.

The great director, Jose Quintero, told a colleague of mine who had written a book on play analysis, "Please teach your students to read a play the way you do." It's an essential skill. But it doesn't have to be complicated. Keep an eye out for the discoveries, the changes, especially from start to finish. What's the story? What happens in the scene? It will serve you well. Look at the balcony scene from *Romeo and Juliet*. They meet one another for the second time and at the end of the scene plan to get married. Whew! Talk about forward movement. Look at the discoveries, the changes. Keep it simple. Take any scene from a well-written play and try it.

So, what are some ways we might go about bringing the play or scene to life?

CHAPTER TEN

WHO IS THIS PERSON YOU ARE BRINGING TO LIFE?

The Character

When Mahershala Ali made his acceptance speech after receiving the 2016 Oscar for the best supporting role in *Moonlight*, he said:

> I want to thank my teachers, my professors. I had so many wonderful teachers. And one thing that they consistently told me—Oliver Chandler, Ron Van Lieu, Ken Washington—is that it wasn't about you. It's not about you. It's about these characters. You're in the service to these stories, to these characters. I'm so blessed to have had the opportunity. It was about Juan. It was about Chiron. It was about Paula.

This statement is power packed with thoughts about the acting process and acting training. By beginning with words of thanks to his teachers, he not only credited them for the techniques they taught him but also acknowledged the importance of their work to his success. He is obviously blessed to have had such extraordinary mentors, and it is encouraging to hear them recognized for the positive work that they do. Although not every teacher of acting is outstanding, I hear more and more about the good ones who are lauded for what they have given their students and who are not always in the most prestigious programs. I am thinking of a very successful actor who went to North Dakota State University. Talking about how much he learned there, he said, "I use what I learned there every day."

Ali, in mentioning those very wise teachers of his who told him that it was not about him, revealed that they gave him a great gift: "Put your focus on the characters you are bringing to life, and not yourself." Aha! "Cherish not yourself in the art, but the art in yourself," says Constantin Stanislavski. It's amazing how easily and often the ego can get in the way of the work. And that work is, as Ali said, serving the stories and the characters, which requires a dogged analysis of the script, energized by a guided use of the imagination.

Defining and bringing to life the person you are playing may very well be the most creative work you do as an actor. As actors grow in their craft and in experience, they tend to focus mostly on the development of character. I had a chance meeting with that wonderful actor, Brian Bedford, and told him how I was looking forward to seeing *Measure for Measure*, in which he was to play the duke at the Stratford Theatre Festival. I also mentioned that I was looking forward to seeing Colm Feore as Angelo in that production. Bedford said, "Well, he has a marvelous part, doesn't he? I have no idea what I'm going to do with mine." I ran into an actor who was rehearsing Martha in *Who's Afraid of Virginia Woolf?* and asked her how the rehearsals were going. In an agitated manner, she said, "I still don't know who this woman is." I wonder if, as an actor matures, the foundational techniques of action, inner monologue, communication, and so on, don't eventually become embedded in his subconscious, while the search for character requires more of his conscious attention.

As I gained some experience as a teacher, I came to believe that it was not too early to introduce the concept of the "who" to young acting students. Although the focus on the basic techniques demands the initial attention, the concept of character definition can be initiated early on. In fact, students cast in their theatre department productions are faced with the need to develop clear-cut characterizations. I have already mentioned how my undergraduate mentor, Otto Kvapil, guided us to vivid and joyous character work in *The Taming of the*

Shrew and what an important lesson it was for me. It changed the way I read plays, even at the beginning of my theater work.

So, how does the actor go about the search for who this person is? As Ali states, you are in the service of these characters, so it stands to reason that you need to begin with a careful examination of the script. The old list of questions: "What does the character do? What does she say? What do others say about her? What descriptions does the playwright provide?" can be the springboard to the search. She does many things in the play. Which are primary? Which are secondary? And which are the result of dominant qualities she possesses that are necessary to tell the story?

Let's look at the character of Anne Frank. She does many things in the play, but certainly her positive spirit, her love of life, her sense of play, her sensitivity to others, are at the heart of the play and explode in its climax. What does she do in that scene? She tries to pull Peter out of his despair. In doing so she reveals her active sensitivity toward others, her love for them, and her proactive approach to Peter's situation. This is a quality she demonstrates throughout the play. She also reveals, in what she says, that she has an absolute love of life, which animates a great spirit in her and touches everybody. And that quality is so essential to the forward movement of the play as we watch the spirit of this wonderful young girl get snuffed out by the forces of evil.

In *Of Mice and Men*, Crooks is an isolated man, and his isolation drives him to have a conversation with another man who will listen, even though he knows that man doesn't comprehend much of what he is saying. Out of his need to connect with someone, he allows himself to reveal some personal things from his past. His personal pride comes out when Lennie enters, and Crooks tells him to get out.

As the actor playing Crooks continues to analyze the script for clues as to who this person is, he can also focus on word choice, that is, the language the character uses, such as repeated words, curse words. (It doesn't always mean the character is angry just because he curses.) What are his mental preoccupations? Where do they come from? What about his background; does it inform the way he now sees life? How bright is he?

We have so far focused on the analytical phase of the process. Now let's put the imagination to work. Doing so usually involves elements which are not so clearly obvious in the text. Recall Eleonora Duse's comment later in her career, in which she recalled playing Juliet when she was a young actor. She said that she analyzed the role a great deal, but if she could do it again, she'd go to Verona and imagine. Let's apply that to our work here.

Anne Frank's dominant qualities, those things that make the script go, are her joy and love of life, her spunk and spirit, her sensitivity toward others, her drive to engage others in fun, her capacity to love, and we see all those qualities in the last scene with Peter, which climaxes the play. But now let's engage the imagination and ask some questions that aren't readily answerable from the mere facts of the script but are relevant to it: What about her fears and how deep are they? Does she believe they will all get out of there alive? What about her sexuality? What happens to her physically in the two years they are living in their hideout? What are her exact feelings about the other characters in the play—Mr. Dussel, her mother, her sister, and so on? Does she ever have any negative feelings? What makes her laugh? What about her capacity to love? What about that school experience? "Mrs. Quack! Quack!" What was that about? What does she like about herself? How does she feel about being bound by these walls where she is forced to live? Are any or all the answers to these questions relevant to the play, and, if so, how?

With Crooks: What happens if they fire him? Where would he go? What is there in this world that keeps him on the job? Is there any danger in talking with Lennie? What is his source of dignity? If his situation is so abject, why doesn't he kill himself? The key here is to ask some questions about the character that emerge from the facts of the script but for which you don't know the answers.

One actor told me that when she played Sergeant Sarah Brown in *Guys and Dolls* she considered the character's sexuality among other things. I thought it was a very creative thing to do. But how does it manifest itself in the script? Well, it would certainly be a factor in the Havana scene, not that she would be a vixen, but she's not an iceberg either. And after all, she does get married to the gangster in the end.

And then, what about any external adjustments you might want to consider? For starters, is there anything in the script that suggests or demands a physical adjustment? Crooks has a bad back. Lennie has power he doesn't know he has. I saw Judi Dench play Viola in *Twelfth Night*, and when that character was faking it as a man, she made a slight adjustment with her foot (turned in) to suggest masculinity. Very slight, but very effective, and very important to the plot, as Orsino must believe that she is a "he." When Tom Courtenay played the lead in *She Stoops to Conquer*, he had a marvelous comic stutter when he came face-to-face with a pretty woman, "maa, maa, maa, maa."

Do you really need to make a physical or vocal adjustment for a role? Shouldn't you just bring your own body and voice to the role and refrain from adding on some unnecessary stuff? I had an actor once who, in playing the stage manager in *Our Town,* wanted to use a New England accent. I disallowed it because, for me, the very reason that Thornton Wilder called the play *Our Town,* and not *Grover's Corners,* was that it was universal and not particular. But it is a natural thing, I believe, for an actor to ask himself what the physicality or vocal quality of this character should be? How does he deport himself physically or vocally? What particularizes him? How does he walk? Talk? Is an adjustment necessary? Onstage, everything looks like a choice, whether it's a conscious choice by the actor or not. Character definition is part of the dramatic experience, so an audience accepts what it sees as who the character is.

Some Exercises in Character Work:

Exercise: In the classroom, or for the actor working alone: Take a character from a very short play and write down the key things that character does or says as well as what others say about him or her, and then try to create a picture of who the person is. Try the first short scene from Arthur Schnitzler's *La Ronde,* with the soldier and the prostitute. Try to define the people from what you know here. Ask yourself what dominant or essential qualities make the script or scene work. Talk it out. Who is this person? What do you know? What can you infer? What do you imagine? What does it take to make the scene work at its most basic level? Find other scenes you like. You can do this exercise with any scene or play you or the class know. Actors need to get into the habit of defining the character.

Exercise: Be aware and make note of how certain stage and film actors portray their characters. I recall being struck by Nicole Kidman's character definition in *The Birthday Girl*; Anthony Hopkins slight madness as Kellogg; Paul Newman's simplicity in *Fort Apache the Bronx*; Mahershala Ali's character in *Moonlight*; Saorise Ronan's innocence in *Brooklyn*; Meryl Streep's characterization in most anything, or Tom Hanks in *The Terminal*. Crista Moore's characterization of Louise in the Tyne Daly version of *Gypsy,* with Wayne State Theater's Bob Lambert as Tulsa, subtle though it was, made me understand why the title was *Gypsy*.

Exercise: Find role models for a role you are doing or might do. Use real people, not actors in movies or stage plays. What specific things, external or internal, do you find that you might use? What about the rhythm and tempo of the character? Is she high-wired, serene, measured? What exactly does she do to give you that impression? The people out in the world are the actor's subjects whom they are studying. Heads up! Try them out in a scene or monologue for yourself or as a classroom exercise.

Exercise: If you really want a challenge, try to figure out exactly who Benvolio is in *Romeo and Juliet,* or Paris for that matter.

Make this all fun for yourself. It's a creative process.

I had the opportunity to direct a play written by a respected colleague of mine. It was a short play about an African American man whose erratic behavior was dangerous enough that the powers-that-be were considering doing some brain surgery on him to "normalize" him. The events of the play were quite clear, but the exact "who" of the main character was more open-ended, and my initial instinct was to let the work of the playwright do the work of the characterization. But, Cliff, the actor playing him said, "This is my story, and I want to tell it the best way we can." After we blocked it, Cliff started to push me in a kindly way "What do you see? Tell me."

Well, the door was opened, and I said, "I think he's so serious all the time. Does he see any humor in life? What makes him laugh?" Well, in the next rehearsal he was "Mister Joy-Boy." He asked me what I saw, and I told him that, but from then on, he was more than just serious. He pushed me again, "What are you seeing?" I said, "He's all aggression. Is there any vulnerability in the guy?" The next rehearsal, he was "Mister Milquetoast." I told him that, and added, "But don't lose it all; try to blend it in." Later, he asked, "What are you seeing now?"

I said, "I don't know how he feels about the other people in this play." Next rehearsal he was making some personal contact that was more complex. On and on it went. He was superbly able to blend all these things into a multifaceted human being. It became truly fun to work this way with an actor who was totally willing to explore and try most anything to get to a definition of who this person was. It was very successful. And it was an object lesson for us both.

Here's an example of the very opposite way of working on character. I was to direct a production of Shaw's *The Misalliance*. During auditions there was one actor, Carley, who clearly knew what to do with the role of the Polish acrobat Lina Szczepanowska, a strong minded, strong bodied, beautiful daredevil. The casting was a no-brainer. Carley was African American, which only bears mentioning here because, though she was obviously not Polish in her look, she knew exactly who this flamboyant woman was and demonstrated it in her audition. Besides which, we did nontraditional casting at the Hilberry and our audiences accepted it and even expected it. Anyway, at the start of rehearsals, I talked to Carley about the role and told her I thought she really knew this character, so "Why don't we, in the rehearsal period, search for some more complex internal qualities and see where that takes us? It is educational theatre after all, so let's get educated." I asked if she was willing to do that, and she quickly agreed.

So, in the rehearsal period we explored opposites, vulnerabilities, relationships to some of the other characters, her sexual attraction to the son, Bentley, and the like. During the first technical rehearsal, while we waited for the designers to complete their tasks, she asked me, "Well, what do you think about where we are now with Lina?" I said, "I think your initial instincts are right for the role, and if it feels right for you, we should go back to that, even though I think that we gained a lot from the exploration. What do you think?" She said, "Yes," and that's what we went with, and she was wonderful in the role.

CHAPTER ELEVEN

CAN I BE HEARD?

The Voice

Up to this point, with the exception of script analysis, I have focused on the internal skills of acting. I do think that selecting an action (intention, goal), using thoughts and images (inner monologue), and connecting with your partner, all with the goal of bringing the scene or play to life, are necessary interior techniques, foundational and achievable for the beginning actor as well as the more experienced one.

But now let's turn to skills that I think of as external, that is, obvious and necessary techniques that an actor will need to both deliver and shape a performance, most particularly vocal and physical skills. If you work in a department that has a voice and movement teacher, then most of this will be taught by her or him. But if this is not the case, what follows can be useful for the acting teacher and can be a good technique for the teacher or director to possess, as well as for the actor working alone.

Sir Ian McKellen has said that the most fundamental technique that an actor needs is audibility. Can't argue that. If I can't hear you, nothing else matters. Two older actors who had studied with Constantin Stanislavski, were asked what exactly they learned from the master, and neither could remember much except that Stanislavski said "Voice! Voice! And more Voice!"

Okay, we got the message. Now how do we get that audibility? The actor needs a voice that has carrying power without sounding like he is hollering, together with resonance to give it a pleasant tone. Both are achievable. If an actor is blessed with a naturally strong, resonant voice, lucky him. I once asked an actor at the Shaw Theatre Festival in Canada what he did to get and maintain the strong voice he had onstage.

He said that he was always the loudest kid in his class, so this big voice was always there. But more often, that strong resonant voice in professional actors is the result of training. I asked the prominent actor, Nicholas Pennell of the Stratford Theatre Festival, about his vocal training. I knew Pennell had studied at the Royal Academy of Dramatic Art in London, and I specifically asked him if he studied with J. Clifford Turner, who was the voice teacher there for many years. Pennell's response was "He literally gave me a new voice!"

Now about Turner. When I took my first full-time theatre job at the University of Wisconsin-Stevens Point, it was a relatively small department at the time. They had a course in their catalogue called Voice and Diction, and I was asked if I would like to teach it. "Well…. I guess." Luckily, I was put in touch with Turner's book, *Voice and Speech in the Theatre*, which basically laid out his approach to vocal technique, including the many exercises he used. Much of the initial voice work was focused on breathing, relaxation, and resonance. I followed his approach and I found it effective the first time I used it, but in my second year there, I had a mature student in my voice and diction class. She was in her early 40s, was a wife and mother, had a small, high voice, and was a very dedicated student, who knew how to work hard. I said to her, "Okay, Diane, I am going to use you as my test case to see if this Turner stuff really works." She applied herself, worked on the breathing, the relaxation, the production of tone and resonance, and at the end of the semester she could basically bounce a full voice off the back wall. Later in the year, she played the lead in a production of *Mary, Mary*, and was able to command the space vocally in a big auditorium. I only tell this story to make the point that this kind of technique is definitely learnable. And, of course, as an actor continues her work over time, her vocal skills become stronger and stronger.

Here are a few more examples before I suggest some exercises in vocal production. The first play I directed at UWSP was *Lysistrata*, and the girl I cast in the lead was right for the role in many ways, but she needed more vocal power to have the command that the role needed. I recall her lying down in the hallway by the rehearsal door and doing some relaxation exercises and then some exercises to get her breath down to her diaphragm, supported, and fuller. She did well in the role, but that was only the beginning. After graduation, she came back to act in our summer theatre. She now had this huge voice, very commanding in the theatre. I asked her how this happened, and she said, "It's all breathing." That's what accounted for the tremendous resonance she had *learned*.

When I directed *A Delicate Balance* at the Hilberry Theatre, I had a mature, experienced actor playing the lead. At one point he had to emit a huge primal wail, which he did frighteningly well. I asked him how he was able to create this sound that filled the theatre with its horror, and he said, "I breathe down to the floor just before I do that."

In my own experience, while playing Henry Higgins in *My Fair Lady*, I paid the price for not supporting my voice properly. In the "Rain in Spain" number, the ending is a wild Spanish vocal release of joy "I...EEEE!" One night, I didn't get the big breath I needed to support my voice for that exultant shout, and my voice got strained to the point where it limited my vocal projection. After that, what could I say but, "lesson learned."

There are many systems of vocal and speech production which have been very successfully employed in various training situations. Kristen Linklater's *Freeing the Natural Voice* has a long history of success. I was quite taken by her approach to the craft. When I was at the Hilberry, one of the graduate actors wanted to do some specialized work on his voice, and he asked me if we could do an independent study on it. I told him I'd always wanted to try out some of the exercise work in Linklater's book, so he and I would go into the theatre on a regular schedule and try them. He laid on the floor and did the relaxing work as well as the vocal work, and it was clear that we made some real progress and discovered some terrific things using her approach. This actor, by the way, has had a full professional acting career and works regularly at the Guthrie Theatre in Minneapolis.

I mentioned at the outset of this section that vocal and physical techniques are in the main, technical, but that is not totally accurate. Of course, there are many technical aspects of vocal production, but there are some sneaky elements that make it more than mere external work.

For example: I had the good fortune to work with Clyde Vinson, a superior voice teacher in New York. In addition to teaching his own acting and voice classes, Vinson was often hired as the vocal coach for Broadway productions. He told me a story of working on a Broadway play with Richard Dreyfuss, who was coming back to do theatre after having done much of his recent work in films and was having some problems with his voice. So, Vinson sat him down and asked him if his problems might not be the result of his coming back to do theatre that he hadn't done for some time, and his concerns about that. Dreyfus admitted that it was, and, according to Clyde, just that open admission freed up some things that were in the way of Dreyfuss's voice. I saw Dreyfuss later in a Broadway play, *Death and the Maiden,* and his vocal command on stage was truly impressive. He had the technique!

Vinson also told me about an actor who was playing Cyrano for the Royal Shakespeare Company when they were in New York. All went well, until the company went to D.C. to continue the run. Vinson got a call that the lead was having voice problems, and would Vinson come down and work with him. What he discovered was that someone came backstage after one of the shows and told the actor that he was having trouble hearing him. That put something in his mind that made him self-conscious and caused him to start having voice problems. Vinson's main job there was to free up the actor to get beyond a comment that set him on a negative path.

If these things can happen to actors at the top of their profession, what does it say about the mental part of this craft? Noel Coward, at the height of his work, was in New York and having voice problems. He went to a coach who had him mooing like a cow. As I said, there are many paths, many ways to go. As the older actors in summer stock would say, "If it works for you." Yes, it all comes down to what works. And with vocal production, the result is all very evident.

Here are a few exercises in relaxation and vocal production that I have found useful and productive:

For relaxation:

- Lie on the floor and release tension in the body by using the tense-release approach. Tense both arms beginning with the hands, make fists and let that tension grow up into the lower arms then the upper arms and let it drive the shoulders up toward the ears. Hold this for a few seconds, and then release, starting with the shoulders, then the upper arms, then the lower arms, and then imagine the tension flowing out of your fingers. Take a breath. Then do the same basic thing starting with the toes, bring the tension up in steps to the buttocks. Then release in steps from the top down. Then tense and slowly release the face, including the jaw, and then the torso. Take a deep breath after each section.

- With partners in a standing position, release the head so that the chin drops to the chest, and allow your partner to place her hands on the sides of your head, firmly, and in complete control, to move your head slowly in unpredictable movements. She must communicate to you that she has total control and won't let your head fall, and that she will tell you when you should take over.

There are many other exercises like this in the Turner, Linklater, and other books. Invent your own, too.

For breathing:

- Following relaxation, focus on your breathing. Vinson used the image of your torso as a bottle as you lie on the floor. Begin by bringing the breath down to the bottom of the bottle which would be the area below your belly button. Continue to bring the breath up, filling up the bottle until you have reached its top at the top of your head. Then release the breath, starting with the top of your head, letting go area-by-area until you have released to the bottom of the bottle.

- Lying on the floor, imagine yourself lying on a beach on a perfect summer day (a nice escape for the Wisconsin students in winter). You have nothing to do today but enjoy the feel of the sun, hear the movement of the water in a nearby lake, and let your body get pulled down by gravity into the sand. Let go totally. Focus on your breathing. Don't try to manipulate it. Watch how it happens. Let your hand move easily so that you place it on your stomach over your belly button. Let the air flow in, starting there, and fill up easily and slowly. Try to take increasingly larger breaths, but not so that you create unnecessary dizziness (hyperventilation).

- Turner has you standing and placing your fingers on your lower two ribs, fingers to the front of your torso, the thumbs to the rear. Draw the breath into these two areas so that your ribs expand outward as you breathe. Hold for five seconds, and then release slowly. This exercise will also help you to let your whole body relax more easily.

- Kneeling with your hands and knees on the floor, draw the breath into your back so that it rises as you breathe in. If you work in pairs, your partner can tell you if he sees your back rising with the intake of air.

- As part of the "like-in-life" approach to acting work, watch a baby breathe. Notice how her stomach rises as she inhales and drops when she releases the air. Also, notice when you are in a big restaurant and a little child starts to scream; he is louder than most everyone else in the room. And he never gets hoarse. Proper breathing plus a deep unsuppressed need makes this happen.

Adding sound to the breath stream:

- With the breath rooted down, begin by adding vowel sounds: *ooo, oh, ah, aye, eee*. Slowly increase volume as you go, while staying relaxed.

- Add words with strong vowel sounds: *box, locks, say, he, Joe*.

- Try a simple piece of text that has strong vowel sounds. Keep the breath down and the body relaxed.

I had a colleague, Shirley Levin, who had earned her theater degree from Carnegie Tech in the late 1940s or early 1950s. She told me a story about the iconic voice teacher, Edith

Skinner, who, at the very beginning of their studies at the university, had each student tape record a paragraph that began, "Once there was a rat named Arthur." My colleague imitated herself on her first recording, a high-voiced, squeaky, small, tight nasal voice. "Hello. My name is Shirley Mae Brown from Pittsburgh, Pennsylvania. Once there was a rat named Arthur..." At the end of the student's four-year program at Carnegie, Skinner had them record the same "Once there was a rat named Arthur..." piece, which Levin demonstrated with a full-voiced, resonant, powerful sound suitable for the Broadway shows in which she eventually appeared. The difference was totally impressive.

CHAPTER TWELVE

CAN I BE UNDERSTOOD?

Diction

"Speak the speech, I pray you, as I pronounced to you, trippingly on the tongue. But if you mouth it as many of our players do, I had as lief the town-crier spoke my lines." That is Hamlet's advice to the players and Shakespeare's take on the necessity of good diction for the actor.

When Len Cariou played Petruchio in *The Taming of the Shrew* at the Stratford Shakespeare Theatre Festival, I truly enjoyed his performance, and I came away thinking how impressive his vocal quality was. I was so impressed with that production that I went back to see the show again, and much to my surprise, I discovered that it was not the vocal power that impressed me but his good, crisp diction. His commanding performance came, in large part, because of his excellent diction, which didn't call attention to itself but was tremendously effective.

When I was at the Hilberry, in charge of the graduate acting students, I asked the artistic director of the Meadow Brook Theatre if she would come to the acting class and respond to some monologues the students were working on. Her feedback to the first actor who had a strong resonant voice was, "Chris, I just came from a staff position at the Oregon Shakespeare Festival, and I cannot hire you because your diction isn't good enough."

In Edward Albee's *Who's Afraid of Virginia Woolf?* in an early exchange between Martha and George, the two leading characters, Martha asks George to make her a drink. He replies that he doesn't suppose that a nightcap would kill either one of them, and Martha says:

Martha: A nightcap! Are you kidding? We've got guests.
George: We've got what?
Martha: Guests. Guests.
George: Guests!
Martha: Yes...guests...people. We've got guests coming over.

Albee goes out of his way to make sure that that tricky sound "*sts*" doesn't make the word sound like "guess." And the actor needs the skill to make it sound like "guests" not "guess." And, that skill requires a kind of dexterity that produces the diction correctly. One British director reportedly asked his actors to "slap the consonants off the back wall of the theatre."

One of the first shows I directed was *The Pajama Game*, and one of the cast members and I had fun with the diction challenges of the show. One of those challenges came in the song "She's Not at All in Love," which got twisted into "She *snot* at all in love." The women in the chorus had to go out of their way to say, "*Shezzz* not at all in love," which brings me to the first basic step in diction—simple awareness.

Diction training begins with personal speech habits, such as regionalisms:
- Substitutions: *since* for *sense, pin* for *pen,* and the like.
- Too much nasality: I come from Cincinnati where the "*a*" in "ask" or "have" can have a strong nasal tone.
- Mispronouncing words: like "*git*" for "get," "*jist*" for "just," and the like. I've watched students using an English accent doing the accent correctly but then saying "git" and "jist."

The next step in awareness is the actual making of consonant sounds for simple clarity. The plosives *p* and *b*, *t* and *d*, *k* and *g*, the fricatives *f* and *v*, *s* and *z*, all need to be clearly articulated for clarity in a theatre. J. Clifford Turner and Edith Skinner have many wonderful exercises for articulation in their books, both of which are available from Amazon. I heartily recommend them for the teacher as well as the aspiring actor. Turner, for instance, has a plosive exercise combined with vowel sounds which goes like this: *oop poo, ohp poh, awp paw, ahp pah, ayp pay, eep pee*. Then the exercise goes on to include the other plosives *b*, *t*, *d*, *k*, *g* with the same vowel sounds. It forces the actor to make all the plosive consonant sounds, and it offers a kind of challenge for him to master.

These exercises are worth the time they take, because they are teachable and learnable. But to learn them requires the actor to "drill, baby, drill," because the technique necessary for good diction is physical dexterity. Turner offers additional exercises, such as the combination of *s* with other consonants, like the "guests" challenge in *Virginia Woolf*. An example is his *s* plus *p* sounds: *oosp, ohsp, awsp, ahsp, aysp, eesp*. And then (get ready) *oosps, ohsps, awsps, ahsps, aysps, eesps*. Continue using the *k* and *t* consonants to replace the *p*.

There are similar exercises for the fricatives *f*, *v*, *s*, *z*. And you can use select scripted material such as: "Amidst the mists and coldest frosts; with stoutest wrists and loudest boasts; he thrusts his fists against the posts and still insists he sees the ghosts." Or "Theophilus Thistle, the successful thistle sifter, in sifting a sieve full of unsifted thistles, thrust three thousand thistles through the thick of his thumb." Or tongue twisters like: "Which is the witch who wished the wicked wish?" "truly rural, purely plural, truly rurally, purely plurally;" "a box of biscuits, a box of mixed biscuits, and a biscuit mixer." There are many others out there. Find ones you like. In my experience, the students take up the challenge of these and have fun with them, and they gain physical dexterity.

CHAPTER THIRTEEN

PLAYING THE MUSIC

Sense and Music in the Language
Making Your Points

I was directing two old pros, excellent actors, in *The Sunshine Boys* at the Attic Theatre in Detroit. I gave a blocking direction to one of them, "Whit, when you say (here I rattled off a line of his dialogue), what if you sat down?" And he jumped in and said, "Is that how you want me to say that line?" I was taken aback. "No, I was just giving a blocking note here." He jumped in again, "But that is a better way to read that line, isn't it?" I said, "If you want to okay, but I wasn't trying to give a line reading. I was just talking about your sitting down. If you want to read it that way though, fine." And he did.

I mention this story here because I almost never give line readings. Oh, if an actor "top-colors" a word, that is, gives it false emphasis, lacks any real inner connection, or performs words or phrases, I would give a note to fix that. But I found that if an actor was working from a true action, a real thought, making an honest, alive connection with her partner, false emphasis or performed language was never much of a problem. Let's look at each of these potential problems:

The action. In the climactic scene of *The Diary of Anne Frank*, Anne says to Peter, "I wish you had a religion, Peter." Her action in the scene is to pull him out of his despair. She offers the idea of adopting a religion as an attempt to give him some peace. That's what she is *doing*. She is not simply saying the playwright's words in some dramatic way, though "religion" is the operative word in that sentence. But the actor needs to find the source of that idea for her so that the idea comes from a real place. She may want to ask herself how she even knows that Peter does not have religion. Has she observed that? Have she and Peter even talked about it? What's Anne's own idea of religion? Is she religious? It may be a stronger choice to imagine that this is the first time that the religion card is on the table. And religion is a very personal choice, so what might go wrong for Anne when she expresses this wish to Peter? The answers to all of those questions are potentially in Peter's reaction to that line.

A noted playwright once said about his work, "I have no idea what the characters are thinking. I only know what they are doing." When the actor makes some decisions about the source of that idea about religion for her, she becomes a big part of the playwriting process. That's what she brings to the table. And yet, the actor does have the responsibility to make the words of the play clear, and yes, even interesting, and she doesn't want to be ignorant of that responsibility.

So, we can begin by asking how words need to have the emphasis, in order to make the meaning clear, and we can, again, start by noticing how this happens in life. We do this instinctually, automatically, when we speak. Emphasis conveys meaning. Listen to others. Listen to yourself. Do it for yourself if you are working independently on your technique. Do it as a class exercise if you wish. And this observation (the technique is always observation) should include the words we stress as well as the words we throw away, almost throw away, or stress less as we build to the word that makes our point. Observe how the best professionals do this. Notice how they don't hang on every word. Notice how they use high notes as well as low notes for the musical flow to create interest. And notice how you do that in life. That's the sense of language you want to bring to your acting work.

And, by all means, bring it to any classical work you might be lucky enough to do. If you stress the wrong words, hang onto set-up words, stress too many words, especially in a line of

Shakespeare, you will make a semiforeign language very difficult to understand. I've read about professional actors who discuss the maximum number of stressed words you can be allowed in a line of iambic pentameter. It's worth considering. Or take any line of Shakespeare and paraphrase it in contemporary language, just to understand the exact meaning for us.

For example, in the opening line of *The Merchant of Venice*, Antonio says "In sooth I know not why I am so sad." We don't talk that way, but if we take that line and paraphrase it in contemporary speech, what might it sound like? Might it be "Honestly, I don't know why I am so sad." What words must have the stress to make the meaning clear? Let's try to distill it further: "Why am I sad?" "Why" and "sad" are essential to make that meaning clear, but if "sooth" or "know not" or "so" or (God help us) "I" get equal stress to "why" and "sad," the meaning begins to get blurred and it falls to the audience to make the meaning clear. We don't go to the theatre to process what's going on. People say, "You have to listen to Shakespeare." No, the actors have to make it clear.

I've subtitled this book *Some Things I've Learned Along the Way*, and one of the most important things I learned was from John Barton in his book, *Playing Shakespeare*. Very near the beginning of that book, he uses the example above from *The Merchant of Venice* to make a point about the use of intention versus "playing a quality." In his video of that book he has his top-flight actors like Ian McKellen, say that opening line with variations, for example, "Do it sadly," then "Do it humorously." And then he asks McKellen to use an intention, for example, to explain himself, or to search his thoughts, or to put an end to the conversation. McKellen does as directed, and the acting is far clearer and sharper. Barton concludes that "There is no doubt that playing the *quality* leads to bad acting." And doing the action is the actor's way to help avoid it.

Let's look at the dialogue from *The Diary of Anne Frank* that follows Anne's line wishing that Peter had some religion.

Peter: No thanks. Not me.

Anne: Oh, I don't mean you have to be Orthodox or believe in heaven and hell and purgatory and things. I just mean religion...It doesn't matter what. Just to believe in something!

Each actor will make inflection choices as she sees fit, most often instinctually, making the rhythm sound like it does in real life for her. But some subtle, even unintended choices can emerge when she begins to act this dialogue. A subconscious sense of the dramatic might cause an actor to give more inflection to the first sentence at the expense of the point which is to "just have some religion," and "believe in something." To fall into that trap is to risk blurring the clarity and even to bring a subtle sense of falseness to that line, and it can really create a problem when she comes to the major dramatic line near the end of that scene: "I still believe, in spite of everything, that people are really good at heart." If every piece of that line, and the others that precede it, all have the same kind of stress, then nothing stands out as the important point.

Again, all of this is very obvious in many ways, but it bears listening to how these things musicalize themselves naturally in everyday speech. Try some classroom exercises of your own invention, if you are the teacher. You might have class members tell personal stories that excite them, and then have the class listen for the inflection patterns that occur naturally. Or better yet, record them, so that the class can follow the story first, and then relisten to it for the stress patterns.

For the individual actor working on her own, listen to these things in life and jot them down. Yes, these are simple, obvious things, but listen to what we throw away and what we stress, and how throwing a line or phrase or word away is not really throwing it away, but merely forming a link from one point to another. Again, when everything is important, nothing is important.

Another **example**: When an acting student has not made the ideas his own and they are still somebody else's words, pronouns at the ends of sentences can get inflected in a way that we don't inflect them when we talk in life. For example: "I don't know, but I'll ask them." That "them" gets diminished a bit when we communicate real ideas, and the verb "ask" is the operative word. Listen carefully for over-stressing pronouns that end sentences.

Another **example** of the music of the language, and the communicating of ideas is the use of the pause. Once again, the sense of the dramatic comes into play here. There's no question that a pause in the right places can create beautiful tension in a scene, and indeed is wonderfully dramatic. But this *o'er done*, can ruin a scene and call attention to itself, or worse, invite inattention. The old axiom is to use the pause judiciously, that is, don't overuse it, because otherwise, it won't be as effective when you really need it. If the pause is filled and necessary and doesn't violate the truth of the moment, then good. But when it merely creates a hole in the moment, it can really break the flow of a scene. One older British actor is quoted as saying to a scene partner, "See here, old man, if you pause right there, I'm going to have to say something." And one way to keep an actor from over pausing is to indeed invite his partner to jump in and say something in an unfilled moment of pause. This interruption can also have the effect of energizing the inner monologue of a scene. The minds must be dynamically engaged rather than letting the acting energy slip into self-focus.

For fun, try to play with some of the pauses in Harold Pinter's work. Pinter has written in the pauses in much of his work, so he seems to be telling the actor what is going on between two people, as well as musicalizing the work at the same time. Some of his pauses are in fact dead air, as he intends them to be, and they indeed occur that way in life; most others are filled with a kind of tension that occurs when a dynamic idea is left hanging in the air. Look at his play, *The Lover* as an example of this. The wife is trying to figure out why her husband is trying to explode the game they have with each other. The air between the two can crackle with energy as the husband rolls out grenades, and waits for them to explode in the pauses that Pinter writes in. Play with this scripted material in class. It's fun to do.

CHAPTER FOURTEEN

WHAT AM I DOING PHYSICALLY?

Movement on Stage; Shaping the Performance

I recently worked with a young man who asked me to look at the audition pieces he had prepared for acceptance into undergraduate acting training programs. He had been the star of his high school productions and was ready to step out into a broader world. He did his first selection and immediately afterward, asked, "What do I do with my hands?"

A friend told me about his experience watching a taping of the TV series *The Newsroom*. On the day he saw it, they were shooting a scene with Jane Fonda, as the owner and big mogul of the whole network operation, who was seated at a conference table asserting her authority over the others. They shot the scene, and the cameraman said to the director, "The hands [Jane's] are too busy." The director told the props person to get her a glass of water and put a pitcher by it. They reshot the scene. Problem solved.

I juxtapose these two stories as an illustration that the demands of physical choices are an ever-present concern of the actor, but of course the seasoned professional has built-in ways of dealing with this.

When I auditioned potential actors for the Hilberry acting company, I developed a note-making code for myself so I could jot down immediate impressions as a guide to the selection of actors. One was "P/A" which meant physically awkward or physically self-aware. Often it was "P/A ½," but still something that pulled my attention. Something we would have to work on in the training process if the actor came on board. I came to believe that most often that physical self-aware quality might have been the result of the actor not having made physical decisions for the monologue, and as a result, that little critic which can sit on an actor's shoulder, might say, "Geez, my hands must look stupid." or "Why is my leg shaking?" or the like. Or perhaps he is not allowing himself to completely enter into the world of the play, inhibiting the free flow of natural physical impulses, and rather subconsciously, keeping the focus on himself as the actor.

At the outset of this book I had the actor ask the question, "What am I doing?" which focused on the internal aspects of acting. In this section, I want to look at the external aspects of the craft, but even in this pursuit, it is impossible to separate the external from the internal. Uta Hagen has said that, "Movement is destination," which makes great sense, and is a freeing skill in a way. I tell the beginning students that there are really only two moves on the stage. I am coming toward you, or I am moving away from you. Oversimplified? Yes. I can stand or sit, turn in or away, make a direct cross, an arcing cross, and so on, but basically, it's all destination.

How do we make those decisions? Well, what does the script tell you? Much of it is right in there. The dialogue suggests that I am going to you. Or away from you, based on how we feel about each other at a particular moment. Look at *The Diary of Anne Frank*: Anne is pressing Peter (but not too much, or she'll lose him). Peter, in the intensity of his feelings and his reaction to Anne's positivism, which he rejects, might move away from her very easily or at least turn away. Does she touch him physically? When? How? If she does, what does he do in response?

Then there is the stage business. In *Our Town*, on the morning of their son's wedding, Dr. Gibbs and his wife sit down to breakfast. She places the plate in front of him, and he exclaims, "Why Julia Hersey. French toast!" She sits down at the table and he reaches for her hand on the table. That's it. No words exchanged. It is very much the reality of that world. The people don't say, "I love you." It is not in their world. A touch of the hand at a highly emotional moment is a big deal. And the playwright gives the direction.

What happens when acting students must prepare scenes for class, but they have to work independently? I can honestly say that this has almost never been a problem, that is, they are perfectly capable of sketching out the physical actions successfully. As we work on the scenes, I might experiment with the physicality of the scene, by adjusting the distance between characters, adding business to vitalize moments or the like.

I think it's fair to say that, in most production situations, it is common for a director to block early on in the rehearsal process. In my case, I preblocked the script, setting down the moves in advance so that the story got told, the actors knew what the setting was, and how they might use it. When I was working with actors for the first time, I would tell them at the first rehearsal that I had preblocked the scene, but I also told them if they felt an impulse to move, to go for it, and I'd try to adjust to it as we went. I also told them that, if we ended up at opening night with all the same moves we started with, we wouldn't have done our jobs. John Jory, the noted artistic director of the Actors Theatre of Louisville, left a set of notes for the person who was to succeed him in that job. One of them was, "If you hire a director and he hasn't blocked the play after the first week, fire his ass."

On a rare occasion, I'd come across an acting student who had no idea at all how to move on stage, and I'd ask myself how I had learned to do that. I concluded that I learned much of it watching those pros when I was a kid in summer stock, as I was running the light board for every performance. Watching good actors inhabit the space with a remarkable ease was such an important lesson for me. So once again, observation is a key component of the learning process. You can learn a lot by watching.

An actor's body is his instrument, as it is so often said, and he needs to have it tuned and ready to respond in as many ways as possible. Keeping that instrument strong, flexible, graceful, energetic and in good health is obviously an important component of the craft. There are many techniques used in acting training programs that can be applied toward improving movement on stage: Alexander, Pilates, Feldenkrais, Rolfing, yoga, dance, mime, combat. The list goes on. It is in the actor's best interest to commit to a technique and embrace it. And yet what are we to make of that superb director Nagle Jackson's comment that many of the best actors he knows and has worked with are physical wrecks? Another paradox of acting, but what serious actor wouldn't want a solid set of physical skills as an essential part of his work?

Some in-class **exercises** to work on the physical aspects of acting are:

- With the whole class sitting in place as the teacher is talking to them about whatever, she can say to the students, "Now I'm going to ask you to do something, and when I say it, I want you to do it with no thought at all. Just do it." And then she says strongly "FREEZE! Don't move. Just FREEZE!" And then she says, "Now what are your hands doing? Look at them. Now imagine yourself on stage with a large audience looking at you. Are you comfortable with the position of your hands right now? Observe how you do things. Are you thinking that "My hands look stupid," or that "I must do something with them?" No. That's the kind of nonthinking about self you want when you are on stage. Make the decision and go with it. "Now adjust your position, make a physical decision, relax with it, don't doubt yourself, and go with it. Adjust your legs and feet." Do the same thing. Make a decision, and then go with it. This is an external way of getting at the physical.

- As a follow-up, consider this: I think that when we are audience members, we subconsciously believe that what we are watching on stage is edited work, that is, that things we are seeing are selected actions (physical as well as internal), and that everything has a dramatic purpose, even though it may also appear to be spontaneous. The selecting of physical actions has a purpose in the work, and paradoxically, can lead to freeing the actor to behave spontaneously, or at least to make it appear so.

- I have included in the Exercises section on page 121 some other ways to address the physical freedom that an actor wants.

- Look at the scene from *The Diary of Anne Frank* from the physical point of view. What's in the space? How might the two people react physically to one another? How close are they? Do they ever touch?

- Look at the first scene from Arthur Schnitzler's *La Ronde* and imagine the physicalization of it: place, entrance, exits, how the two characters relate to each other. Look at this as if you were having to stage it for yourselves for a class project without the help of a director.

Hamlet cautions the actors in his advice to the players, "Nor do not saw the air too much with your hand thus, but use all gently, for in the very torrent, tempest, and, as I might say, whirlwind of your passion, you must acquire and beget a temperance that gives it smoothness." This, I believe, is Shakespeare telling us about the need for technique that takes physical work beyond mere unbridled passion and making good physical choices to shape the scene.

Lynne Kadish, Ken Umland
A Delicate Balance
Hilberry Theatre
Wayne State University

Antonette Doherty, Dwight Tolar
Abelard and Heloise
Hilberry Theatre
Wayne State University

Erik Gratton
A Tale of Two Cities
Hilberry Theatre
Wayne State University

Erman Jones, Peter Prouty
Of Mice and Men
Hilberry Theatre
Wayne State University

Cynthia Dozier, Richard Gustin,
Chemin de Fer, Hilberry Theatre
Wayne State University

William Akey, Mary Elder
St. Joan, Hilberry Theatre
Wayne State University

Auntie Mame, Set Design by Russell Smith
Hilberry Theatre, Wayne State University

PART THREE
OTHER USEFUL TECHNIQUES AND EXERCISES

CHAPTER FIFTEEN

But It Should Be Fun; Letting Go; Enjoying It All

Dick Cavett told a story about his making a commercial, and after the rehearsal, the director said, "Now have fun with it!" Cavett did it again and at the end said a disconnected, "Wheeee!"

All of the focus so far here has been on trying to offer some ways to go (techniques) as an approach to acting that is systematic, practical, and workable. This can lead to a serious trap in the work. Yes, it takes effort to acquire necessary techniques, but we must be careful not to let that effort trap us into a slavishness to techniques of working that become ends in themselves and take the joy out of the work.

I was directing a production of the musical revue, *Cole*, featuring the music of Cole Porter, and even though I had very good actors in the cast, there was an uptight feeling about the work as we rehearsed. Everyone was trying very hard to be wonderful in it, but the rehearsals had the feeling of, "Oh my God, we are doing a musical!" The revue had pieces of dialogue and witticisms in between the songs, so one day at a dress rehearsal run-through, I started to laugh uproariously at some of the amusing comments of dialogue, and I urged the assistant director to do the same. We pounded the chairs as we doubled over with laughter. This loosened the cast up. They started to add their own jokes in the dialogue and began to have fun with it. Laughter solved the problem, and we had a good, good show.

In *A Practical Handbook for the Actor*, the authors include in the nine points for selecting an action, that it should be fun, and the fun should carry over to the process of working on a scene or a production.

George C. Scott has said that he liked working with Mike Nichols because he made the process a fun experience. Judi Dench writes that she believes acting should all be fun and full of good humor and prizes that in the process. Nichols once said to his cast, "We're all being so professional here." Meaning, I think, put some joy in it. Tyrone Guthrie stopped an early blocking rehearsal with, "Isn't it a joy to be putting on a play!"

It has often been said that, as kids, we loved playing "let's pretend." I see it in my seven-year-old granddaughter now. There's a basic sense of fun in playing waitress and chef as she takes our orders and serves us our Play-Doh goodies. That feeling of the joy of playing can go away as we grow up. But for the actor, that sense of playing continues. There's just a kick in inhabiting an imaginary world, living the relationships in it, taking the emotional journeys in it, difficult though they may be, and all the aspects of dressing up as someone else, and then showing all of that to whomever will watch.

As an actor matures in her craft, this joy of revealing the character can extend itself into something more complex. Meryl Streep, on the Actor's Studio program, mentioned how she loved revealing the fullness of a person she was playing, and a good example of this was her performance as Florence Foster Jenkins, that special woman who had limited singing ability but enough faith in herself to end up singing at Carnegie Hall. Streep revealed to us the interior world of that person, which is another example of the actor playwriting. It's not unlike what Tennessee Williams did with Blanche DuBois in *A Streetcar Named Desire*. I have always thought that, if I met Blanche in real life, I might have found her annoying and bothersome. But in William's hands, she becomes a sympathetic person.

Okay, but how do you do fun...or teach fun? For the teacher, fun may be generated early on in the form of some exercises that are not script-related but merely serve to free up students, sending them the message that it's okay to let loose, let go, and do some spontaneous things that ultimately have a relationship to some of the basic techniques we have been learning.

Loosening-Up Exercises

- For example, simple warmups that loosen the body, such as shaking the legs, the arms, the head, the buttocks, with instructions to "just do them" without any right way to do it. Then bring in the imagination.

- Tell the class you're going to call out various things that you want them to be and when you call them out, the students are to immediately do them without thinking or planning what to do. Just do it. Don't watch others. Do it in your own unique way. Emphasize that this is not a performance. Then call out: "Shake like a belly dancer; like a dog that has just come out of the water; like a person who is freezing; like a person who is shocked; like a person who's got religion; like a hula dancer; like a paint mixer." Add your own.

Slow-Motion Exercise

- Tell student to play their favorite sport as if they were the greatest baseball, tennis player, and so on. Or tell them to dance like the world's greatest ballet dancer, Fred Astaire, or Ginger Rogers, someone who is having his feet being shot at, or someone who is being tickled—all in slow motion. Add your own physical activities.

There are many of these exercises, with multiple goals, the first being to send the message that it's desirable to do seemingly wild and crazy things here, to use the imagination to trigger the whole body, to allow yourself to let go. Hey, it's play time! Free yourself up. Enjoy yourself. The underlying goal is to connect the imagination with the physical and to just let go and enjoy it. In my experience, students were quite ready and willing to throw themselves into this.

Another way of bringing the fun into it all, is to make the world of the play as vivid, real, compelling, and moving as possible.

- With this approach, we let the script lead us to the fun of it all. Start with the character you are playing. It is dress-up time! Time to crawl into the skin of someone else, dress like them, think like them, walk and talk like them, see the world as they see it, create the drives and needs they have, and then show that to the world. Where else can you do this?

- Look carefully at what the playwright gives you. Turn your imagination loose on this, and then enlarge it if you can. Embrace this person. Try to excite yourself about her. If you are playing Anne Frank, find that joy of life she has in yourself and let it fly, the joy she has when she gives gifts on Hanukkah to each person in the room. And her love for Peter. What excites her about him? Is she sexually attracted to him? What are her thoughts? How does she think? What doubts and fears does she have? How does she feel about things, about the people in her life, like her mother for instance? Make it specific and give your imagination the freedom to lead the way.

Make the connections personal.

- In plays, you are expected to interfere with the other person. You have the freedom to do it, unlike in life. It's playtime, so let yourself go as you interact with your partner. It goes farther than mere performance, though that is important too. Try for a real interaction: loving, hating, arguing, questioning, whatever. Do it. Allow it to be real. Feel the interaction leap alive and enjoy that. From the moment that Anne Frank enters Peter's bedroom in the last scene of the play, their reaction to the fight they both witnessed between Peter's parents is personal. They are both deeply shaken by it. There is an interaction before the dialogue even starts. They are pulled into each other's energy field. That should be fun for the actor, if not for the character.

An exercise for this is one I called "silent communication."

- Actors work in pairs, seated cross-legged opposite one another on the floor and make open connections with each other without speaking. The teacher hands one of the actors a card with a message to send out to the other…silently, for example, "Hold me," "Don't leave me," "You disgust me," "Go away," "I can't believe you just said that!" Find your own messages. Use big moments in plays you know, and then boil down the reactions to a specific line for use in the silent communication. Want to see how it works? Watch Viola Davis in *Fences* when Denzel Washington as her husband tells her "I'm gonna be a daddy [by another woman]."

Live your ideas and images and enjoy them too.

- Make them your own, because they are. Select ones that ring your bell. Send them out and watch them land on someone else. That can be fun, even when the ideas are negative.

- **As an exercise**, tell the group to relate a personal experience story that excites or interests them. Have the other people in the group watch the face of the storyteller, looking for the ideas and images to emerge. Or have them read a limerick to spring a joke or make a point at the end. Make it fun for yourself and the others, too.

Enjoy the release of your emotions whatever the context of the play.

In a weird way, the actor's emotional release is part of his job, and when he hits it right on, there's a satisfaction that can occur. When Anne says to Peter, "When I think of the love of you, dear Peter," that emotional release has to be satisfying for the actor as well as for the character. It's down deep. It's not what Anne is necessarily trying to show, but for the actor, it can feel positive.

- **Here's an improvisation exercise on this point.** It's based on the concept that we define the character we are playing in part from how other people treat us in life, for example, your lover, your parent, your boss, your child. How they relate to us can tell us who we are to them. So, select a pair of students to do the improvisation, one of whom knows the relationship, and one of whom doesn't. A situation I used was: Two brothers. One, Frank, was sent to jail because of the other, Harry. Frank has come to get his revenge on Harry. He does this by producing a gun, placing it on the table, and, without saying so directly, wants Harry to pick up the gun and blow his own brains out. In the improvisation, the actor playing Frank knows who he is and what the relationship is; the actor playing Harry does not know who he is or what the relationship is. The actor playing Frank must communicate to the actor playing Harry, without any obvious and overt reference to the situation, what Harry has to do. Sounds difficult, doesn't it? But two first-year actors can make it work beautifully.

Exercises related to a specific acting technique.

These last few exercises are classroom ones that can free up the actor to play and create, each related to a specific acting technique, but much of the fun can happen within the script. Oh, of course, there are real practical things that must be addressed first: learning lines, setting the moves, doing the interior work, selecting actions, and so on, but even in the case of *The Diary of Anne Frank,* doing the research, for example, seeing a picture of the actual room in which the family lived for two years can be a helpful feeling experience for the actor.

So, make it fun for yourself.

Work, yes, but fun work. I think back to one of my early experiences acting in *The Taming of the Shrew.* During auditions, I could see that the director was leaning toward me for the role of Lucentio and that he had three women in mind for Bianca, Lucentio's love interest. The three girls were all good-looking, but one was especially attractive to me. As the auditions proceeded, I kept thinking, "Oh, please cast her. It would make it so easy for me to act with her in that role." Well, he did, and I got to "pitch woo" to this woman who rang my bell. And this happened only onstage when we were acting, because she was in fact engaged to the actor playing Baptista.

Sometimes the work on a role in rehearsal, with all its complexities, the self-doubt, the performance pressure, the expectations, can generate a lack of freedom and seriousness that become counterproductive and need to be addressed. An interesting story about that comes from the Stratford Shakespeare Festival in Canada. The wonderful actor, Marti Maraden, was rehearsing the role of Cecily in *The Importance of Being Earnest*. The artistic director, Robin Phillips, was directing it. At one point in rehearsal when Maraden had a chunk of dialogue, Phillips stopped the rehearsal and said, "Marti, your hair is driving me crazy. Here, take these bobby pins and pin it up, please, and do the speech as you are doing it." Well she did, and reportedly it released all kinds of wonderful, truthful, comic things that made it leap to life. The people in the room recoiled in laughter and applause, and that device was then referred to by the Stratford actors as "a hairpin." "I need a hairpin here." In other words, "Free me up. Release me to live this moment." *

The most basic thing that actors do is to inhabit an imaginary world, in which they appear to behave honestly for the entertainment of other people. In order for the audience to believe what they see, the actors must try to believe it themselves. To make this happen, they use internal and external techniques that allow them to live in the world of the play. Barry MacGregor of the Shaw Theatre Festival in Canada told me a story of how they rehearsed comedies at the festival. There was to be no laughing during the rehearsal. Actors were focused on bringing the play to life, focusing on the reality of it all, and laughter in the rehearsal room seduced them into making it a performance. Barry said that, at the first preview with an audience, when the first laugh came, he found himself annoyed, even upset with that response, until he was reminded of what they were there to do. They were pros after all and knew how to blend the two demands of the work. And I think it's fair to say that the ultimate *fun* is when all this comes together.

Editor's Note: When reminded about this incident, Marti Maraden added "…the 'hairpin' unquestionably became part of the code in Robin Phillips' time and its purpose was to help an actor not to over-consciously deliver a comedic line, but rather to let it land obliquely. Of course, this was meant to broadly suggest an actor could focus on any physical activity to avoid overplaying comedy. It could be leafing through a book or knitting or polishing one's glasses, etc."

CHAPTER SIXTEEN

OTHER USEFUL TECHNIQUES AND EXERCISES

Anyone who has taught beginning acting for the first time has probably asked herself, "Where do I start?" She may see in her students' work physical awkwardness, small voices, fuzzy diction, self-awareness, a lack of honesty in the work, lack of inner connectedness, lack of physical freedom, inability to immerse themselves in imaginary worlds, on and on. She is also most likely to see that some students are initially more gifted than others, and they are sometimes referred to as "having talent." What I learned along the way was that often the students who were initially "not as talented" became the better actors after four years, because they had learned how to use the techniques that made them better actors, while some of their initially talented but less-driven cohorts did not.

For me, the work on scripted material proved to be the most successful way to teach the basic skills, the ones that I had come to believe in and had seen work, measurable skills that were immediately applicable to scripted work. But before I learned this, I spent a considerable amount of class time on what I now consider secondary skills, ones that are very important to the work but are a step removed from the scripted ones. I continued to teach these techniques but spent less time on them, introducing the students to them so they could explore and drill them on their own. Some of these secondary skills include relaxation, concentration, sensory awareness, physical freedom, the connection between the imagination and the body, improvisation, group connection, and others.

For Relaxation: Read Constantin Stanislavski's chapter on relaxation in *An Actor Prepares*. The goal here is to practice relaxing so that in moments of performance tension, the actor can subconsciously let go of unnecessary tension that calls attention to itself, inhibits free movement, drains energy, and creates awkwardness. Most actors can tell stories of doing an audition, for instance, and discovering their leg suddenly bouncing up and down, their shoulders riding up, their jaw or stomach tightening, and the like.

Some exercises for relaxation are:

- Lie on the floor and relax as outlined on page 121.

- Include the imagination in this exercise. Imagine being on the sand by a lake on a perfect day. Hear the water moving, feel the heat of the sun, the breeze. Release. Let go.

- As partners, let one partner lie on the floor and release totally. The other partner picks up one arm of the relaxed person. He should feel dead weight from the person who is totally relaxed. With partners standing and facing each other, one person drops her head down, while the partner takes her head in his hands, and moves it around very slowly in an unpredictable pattern. It should feel as if the one doing the moving has total control, and, most importantly, tells his partner when to take back the control. The one being manipulated must trust that the mover is protecting her.

- As a group, in a circle, turn in profile and massage the shoulders of the person in front of you while you are being massaged by the person behind you at the same time.

- Individually, you can do the first two solo to acquire these skills for yourself.

For Concentration:

The goal here is to strengthen your skill of concentration so that when the audience is pulling your attention, you can stay focused on the world of the play. Many things in life demand our concentration. It takes concentration to drive a car, make a new recipe, do some computer tasks and many others. And it certainly takes an extra amount of concentration when you are acting and being observed by others, when self-consciousness can become an issue. Stanislavski devoted a chapter to concentration in *An Actor Prepares*. Anything an actor can do to intensify her power to concentrate will serve her well.

A first and important step is for the actor, through her imagination, to bring the elements of the world of the play to life, so that they can compel her attention. In the case of *The Diary of Anne Frank*, Anne's focus on Peter at the very top of the last scene, the torture he is experiencing, and her relationship to him, can pull her into that world in an intense way. In the Crooks scene in *Of Mice and Men*, Crooks's connection to Lennie, what he sees, what he imagines him to be, what he needs from him, are the focus of his concentration. The more specific and enlivening that is, the better for the actor.

Some exercises for concentration are:

- In a class, students sit in a circle and the first student says a word, any word. The next person adds a word not related to the first one, and this continues around the complete circle. Then any brave soul tries to repeat the group of words. Then another, then another.

- In a class, one person is given a column of numbers to add while other people try to distract him by doing their own phony addition for example, "one and five are six carry the two," just to mess him up.

- "Disobeying hands." Raise one arm out straight before you, then up in the air, then to the side straight out, then straight down by the leg. In the process, the opposite arm follows the pattern one step later, so that when the first arm is up in the air the opposite arm is straight out.

- Say the alphabet backwards while people are listening to you.

- Walk with a book on your head while people are watching you.

- Make up exercises of your own, for example, complex things to do while others watch you.

- Observe yourself in life in moments which demand your strict attention. Notice what you do under those circumstances. What takes place? You will need at least that much concentration when you are performing.

For Physical Freedom:

The goal here is to free up the body, and to loosen it up for free and smooth movement on stage. Think of the body as a positive thing rather than something that creates a negative self-image, which limits rather than expands. Something that adds to the acting rather than subtracts from it. Here the goal of the exercises is to let go, as well as playing; it's okay to do this. There's no right or wrong. Just jump in and do them. Enjoy yourself. As I matured in my teaching, I did fewer and fewer of these, just enough to let them know that it's okay to play, and that it is part of the craft.

Some exercises in physical freedom, which is a continuation of some of the exercises in having fun, and include the use of the imagination:

- In class, the teacher calls out something and the students just do it immediately, no thinking allowed. Use the whole body. Jump like a frog, kangaroo, person on a pogo stick, moon walker, basketball player, someone whose feet are being shot at, a person on a trampoline, a ballerina, a cheerleader; jump for joy! Make up some of your own.

- Kick like a football player, a Rockette, a wild horse; add your own.

- For more imagination, tell students to embrace the wind, stop the walls, walk on a tightrope, juggle, draw a circle with a pencil on their nose, or bounce off elastic walls.

- Walk like an elephant, an old person, Miss America, Charlie Chaplin, an ape, you're on the moon.

- "Marionettes." The teacher calls out the moves from above: "Your body is a marionette." The imaginary puppeteer jerks up the right arm and hand (string tied to the right wrist, left wrist, on and on.) Make up your own moves.

- Throw a baseball, snowball, beach ball, Nerf ball, iron ball, balloon filled with water, mud ball.

For Sensory Awareness:

I know acting classes can get a bad rap on this one, as in the song "Nothing" from *A Chorus Line*, but sharpening the senses, like sharpening the concentration, can be very useful for the actor. I mentioned vitalizing the world of the play in such a way that the actor gets pulled into it, and the keenness of the senses is a big help in doing that. Looking and really seeing, listening and really hearing, touching and letting it affect you, using recalled smells to stimulate the senses—all of these are aids to help pull the actor into the world of the play. As noted before, seeing a picture of the actual room where the characters in *The Diary of Anne Frank* was set can be a terrific springboard into that play.

For Crooks, in *Of Mice and Men*, the smell of the barn lean-to where he lives, as well as the sound of the horses that he tends can all, when recalled, help to make that world come more vitally alive for him. Even with the most complete stage set, you can't see the total environment, but you can imagine, and the more specific your work is, the more it is likely to affect you. How much class time is spent on sensory awareness varies from teacher to teacher, but I think it's important for students to know the value of bringing the things in the imaginary world to crackling life, and much of that can come from actors with very alive senses. The sensory world that surrounds the actor becomes believable and affecting for him, so he can affect the audience.

Some exercises in sensory awareness:

- Lie on the floor and see how many actual sounds you can hear. Count them. Do the same thing at the shopping mall, or wherever else you might choose.

- Do the same thing seeing colors: How many can you identify? Label them. Imagine you are creating names for paint samples; what would you call them?

- For a class, I went to the costume shop and got swatches of various materials, then put them under a cloth for the students to feel and identify.

- In a class, have students lie on the floor while the teacher makes various tiny sounds, like opening and clicking closed a pocket-knife, tapping keys on a chair.

- For remembering the feeling of weight, with an imaginary pitcher of water in one hand, and an empty glass in the other, pour the water from the pitcher into the glass. Did your muscles adjust to the change of weight from one to the other?

- Look at something going on far off that interests you. Did your eyes adjust as they do when you really do that? Recall the earlier example of the director who said, "Actors don't look out of windows well." Hear the demand for the imagination to go to work.

- Look at your partner and examine him. Look again more carefully. Did you discover anything new?

Improvisation:

As I've mentioned earlier, improv is certainly a useful skill or technique for an actor to have, and though I leaned on it a lot in my early teaching, I came to use it more selectively as I got more experience in the classroom. I found it most effective in bringing life to a scene or monologue where performance choices, for example, lines and movement, however slick, became ends in themselves and lacked an in-the-moment vitality. I would add another actor to a monologue and take her aside to give her directions on ways to present an obstacle to the monologue actor. Initially when I started working that way, it was my plan to provide an obstacle for the monologue actor (M) to push against to vitalize his work. I might for example, whisper to the obstacle actor (O), "Let him see how much he is hurting you," or "Don't take his nonsense here," or "Stick up for yourself," or "Just walk away if he doesn't convince you," or "Just start laughing," all of these directions coming from the needs of the scene itself.

What I came to realize was that this also became an improv, because the givens were now being adjusted, and M had no idea what O was going to do, like in life. So, it was an improv without M having to create new dialogue, which is properly the province of the playwright. O might make physical adjustments, mental or emotional adjustments, relationship adjustments, even inject a word or line of dialogue of her own. I found that this approach, while bringing the work to life, also communicated to the actors that this kind of spontaneity was what we were shooting for as a main goal in our work. I should add that I only did this when it was needed, and in keeping with the relationships, goals, events of the scene as laid out by the playwright, never just as an exercise in improvisation.

I recently saw an interview of the Motown star, Smokey Robinson, on PBS. When asked if he ever got tired of singing the same songs, he said that he'd sung his songs a thousand or more times, but that every time he sang one, it was new to him.

That echoes an acting philosophy of the famed American actor, William Gillette, who talked about, "The Illusion of the First Time." Robinson said that when people asked him after a show to go to a party, he would say, "I just have been at a party (the performance); now I just want to go home, kick back, and watch TV." I found that when I am searching, as I always am when teaching, things like the Smokey interview pop up and dovetail into the very thing I am working on, in this case, being alive and in the moment "for the first time."

CHAPTER SEVENTEEN

PERFORMANCE SENSE

The actor was playing a blind burglar in Murray Schisgal's *All Over Town*, and he had to come swiftly down a flight of stairs that turned a right angle halfway down to the stage floor. He asked me, "What if I came down the first half and when I hit the middle turn, I somersaulted over the railing to the stage floor?" I said, "Will it be safe?" He said "Yes, absolutely." So, I said "Go ahead. Try it." He did, and the audience screamed with laughter.

Another actor, playing the wealthy, restrained father of a prospective bride, paid a visit to the home of the semi-Bohemian Auntie Mame in the play of the same name. The furniture all reflected the taste of the free-wheeling Mame, with chairs sloped and very low to the floor. The father of the bride sat in one, slowly and cautiously, then tried to cross his legs, but his crossed leg kept sliding down to the floor. The audience howled with laughter.

Michael Shurtleff in *Audition* writes that so many actors are afraid of being too melodramatic, but he responded that he wished he saw more melodrama and romance.

I cite these examples of what I consider a "performance sense," because much of the talk so far has been very much rooted in leading the actor toward an inner truth in her work. But then there is the reality of shaping the performance for just that—performance. The director, who is responsible for telling the story and moving it forward, might tell the actor to face out at a particular moment, or the actor's performance sense will know that, at that moment, the audience needs to see her pain. It's weird in a way, but that's what we came to the theater to see and experience. In *Fences,* when Troy tells his wife that he's going to be a daddy by another woman, we need to see his wife's reality, her pain. How? Where?

When to sit, when to stand, when to be loud, when to speak softly, when to pause, when to go faster, when to release the emotion, when to hold it in (and be able to communicate that), when to turn away, when to remain still, when the emotional response must be strong, all of these elements must work together to shape the performance so that it engages the audience.

Does all this mean you must sacrifice your sense of basic truth when you make performance choices? No, but you'll need to do both basic truth and performance choices at the same time. Can that be done? Certainly. You must learn the lines. You must do some movement on stage, even if strictly speaking, in real life, you'd not move around quite so much in this living room, in this situation. The interior question, "What am I doing?" applies to the physical line, too and must be addressed whether the blocking is organic or set down by the director or a combination of both. But making physical choices and finding pieces of business can be fun, too, and, as long as they are rooted in reality and are consistent with the script, you will be on safe ground.

It must be loud enough so they can hear. "Speak up!" It must be lit enough so they can see. "Get in your light!" "Where is the hot spot of that lamp?" "This is important information here, so make sure it's clear when you say it." So much of performance shaping is just plain common sense, plus creativity.

CHAPTER EIGHTEEN

TERMINOLOGY: Some Things I Learned

Early on, I discovered that using an inexact word to an actor I was directing could send him off on a totally wrong tangent. I realized that I wasn't always as clear as I needed to be. As a result, I became more careful about the words I chose, and sometimes, when I was giving notes, a little voice told me not to give that note because it wasn't clear enough and would only confuse an actor or make her unsure about a moment, so I'd refrain from giving that note.

Terminology in acting can drive us all crazy, because there are so many terms that are used for the same technique. A prime example for that is the word for what Constantin Stanislavski calls "objective," or at least it is so translated in *An Actor Prepares*. See what I mean? We have "objective," "intention," "goal," "essential action," "what are you fighting for?" or, the one that I came to use that I believe came out of the Group Theatre, "action." I like it because it demands *doing something*. Eventually I began asking, "What are you doing?" even though I still hung onto the word "action," as I mentioned in the beginning of this book.

Michael Shurtleff, in his book, *Audition,* formulated his version of this with a question: "What are you fighting for?" I sense that he used that term to generate some dynamic action in the pursuit of the objective, goal, intention. I found this appealing, and for a while I used that term in class. By then I found the terms, "objective," "intention," "goal" too coldly analytical, leading to heady acting and not lifelike art.

CHAPTER NINETEEN

RESPONDING TO A SCENE OR MONOLOGUE GIVING NOTES

For the Teacher

Very early in my teaching career, I was giving notes to a student after she had just done her monologue. She was a bit older and more experienced than the other students in the class and more honest than the others. As I was giving my notes, I felt like a critic rather than a coach. My notes seemed more generalized about emotions, character qualities, even some picky things about physicality and the like. I felt that I wasn't helping much at all, that what I was giving her wasn't of much use. I can still see her. She received my notes with good grace, but I don't think either of us found them satisfactory.

As I grew as a teacher, I learned to focus my notes on the skills we were working on in class, such as, "What are you doing?" (action, need) "Why?" (need), "What's stopping you?" (obstacle), "How do you feel about the other person?" (relationship), and other core techniques. If there was a need for physical adjustments, or even vocal ones, I'd mention those and suggest solutions for them. And, of course, after the first time the actor presented the monologue or scene, we'd need to spell out the who, what, when, where, why of the selection, bringing us all up-to-date on that and being certain that the actor had these solidly in mind.

When Uta Hagen taught her classes, her first response to a scene usually was, "Now, what can you tell me?" She was striving to empower the actor to take charge of her own technique and how it was used in the work she just did. For me, working often with beginning students, I might frame that question as, "Did you do what you wanted to do?" A response might be, "I kept going up on my lines, but I had them when I did them in my apartment," which was a chance to suggest to him that he might try to do the monologue for a friend or fellow student. For more advanced students, a response to that question would usually be more tied to technique.

Usually these questions led to some discussion of what the action might be. I recall one of these discussions that went on for some length with a young woman who was doing a scene from *The Children's Hour* by Lillian Hellman. After we searched for what the action might be, examining the scene and what was going on in it, we settled on what it was, and started discussing something else. But she raised her hand and asked, "Do you think that's the best action for that scene?" I said, "Well, maybe not. What do you think? What else might it be?" And she nailed it with a much better choice. I don't mean to give the impression that classes were mere head trips, just that searching was part of the process and that the teacher was not necessarily the font of all wisdom. The real goal was to find the best, useable choice, to give the student the best action to do.

When I had the special opportunity of watching Hagen conduct her class, I tried to match wits with her after a scene. I imagined how I might react to that scene, and then asked what she had to say. I found it very instructive, and I was always pleased when she and I were on the same page. I always learned something as I watched the scene through her eyes. The learning never stops.

I invited the wonderful, former Hilberry actor, Phyllis Somerville, to my class and asked her if she would give notes on the scenes. Her first response was, "I'm not a teacher," but I nudged her into it, since I am always interested in what actors I admire see and have to say about the work of others. What Somerville commented on in many of the scenes was the need for transitions from unit to unit. What I took from that was that she was not seeing the actual mental shifts from one major thought to the next (inner monologue/thoughts). Very instructive, and especially important considering the source.

A friend who is a producer at an outdoor Shakespeare Festival here in Royal Oak, Michigan, asked me to come and give notes after one of the *Hamlet* rehearsals he was directing. I did, gave him the notes, explained them, and left it at that. He told me a few days later that he gave them as if they had come from him. My response was, "Good. I was hoping you'd do that." Who cares who gets the credit, as long as it helps the actor and the production? My other response was, "Did those notes do any good?" He said they did.

For the Actor
Responding to His Own Work

Uta Hagen used to say that it is common for actors who have just finished a scene in production to come off stage and exchange words about how it went. Did they nail it? Did they not hit the high spots? Did they find something new in it? Did it come alive or not? Did I give you what you needed? Even technical things. Her point was that actors do evaluate their own work in the absence of the teacher or director, but the audience, in most cases, is the best teacher of all. So, this business of "response" doesn't solely rest with an outside presence. The big thing is, can the actor identify and adjust what needs to be adjusted and keep what needs to be retained? But a word of caution here. Please, actor, don't be checking your technique while you are performing. You came here to play the game. Play it. Be there in the moment and evaluate later.

Finally, do read Michael Shurtleff's classroom analysis of the scene between Amanda and Laura from *The Glass Menagerie* in his book, *Audition,* if you want to see an insightful response to acting work. There is much to learn from it.

CHAPTER TWENTY

WHAT IS ACTING?

This morning I awoke with a fantasy, a flight of my imagination. It was triggered by an interview I saw last night on PBS in which Jeffrey Brown interviewed Kenneth Lonergan, who wrote and directed the Oscar-nominated film, *Manchester by the Sea*. In the interview, there were a few brief clips from scenes, one of which was the final scene between Michelle Williams and Casey Affleck, who meet by chance after an absence of some time. They are former spouses who have divorced after a horrendous accident has driven them apart. She has remarried, has a child, and gone on to a life of her own. He has grown bitter, angry and withdrawn from much of the world. In this scene, it is clear that she, for whatever reason, would like to reconnect with him, and the scene ends with her asking him if he would like to go to lunch sometime. He declines.

Okay, so what is my fantasy? I imagine I am teaching an acting class and I have a DVD of that film and a screen to project it on for the class. I play the scene between Williams and Affleck so we can all get pulled into the drama of it. Then I replay just the last few moments of the scene and ask the students to watch her eyes when she asks him, "Would you like to go to lunch sometime?" Then I replay it again and ask them to do the same thing. I ask them, "What did you see? Look at her eyes, which reveal the inner world of a person filled with an anxiety, risk, even fear." We then discuss what we saw. I want to be sure that they see the deep and honest anxiety she has before he answers the question, fearful of his response. I want them to see the dynamic connection between them, particularly from her end, and the power she gives him in the scene, when, in fact, it is she who, in her new life, should be more secure than he. Look at the deep need she has to make the connection with the simple line, "Would you like to go to lunch?" Now imagine that you just received that script. The line is just a simple question, "Hey do you want to get together?" But Williams has seemingly put her whole being into this moment.

In the beginning of this book I mentioned my "Saint Paul moment" being onstage with Luther Adler, being in the magnetic energy of his look, and saying to myself, "Oh, that's what acting is." Cut to the present, and I can say the same of witnessing what Williams does with that scene. Does that mean that the students can just begin to do what she has done? No, probably not, but they can, if they watch carefully, get an idea of what the goal of great acting can be. We are watching the art at its finest. And we must recognize and prize it when we are in its presence. In performances like these, we can see how the actor can become part of the playwriting process. Lonergan alluded to that in his interview. He talked about watching good actors bring life to his script in a greater dimension than he had originally imagined, and how vital that is to the ultimate creation.

Thomas M. Suda, Cheryl Williams,
Charles Jackson in *All Over Town*
Hilberry Theatre
Wayne State University

Nira Pullin, LeWan Alexander
in *Cole* Hilberry Theatre
Wayne State University

Maribeth Monroe
in *Cabaret*
Bontstelle Theatre
Wayne State University

Anne Adcock, Vickie Schmitt
in *Cat Among the Pigeons*
Bonstelle Theatre
Wayne State University

Brenda Baker
Guys and Dolls
University of
Wisconsin--
Stevens Point

Chris Bohan
Side Man, Hilberry Theatre
Wayne State University

Aaron Moore, Nick DePinto, *Misalliance*
Hilberry Theatre, Wayne State University

Misalliance Set Design by Fred Florkowski
Hilberry Theatre, Wayne State University, *Photo Rick Beilaczyc*

Cast of *The Grapes of Wrath* Hilberry Theatre (1992)
Young girl on top of truck: Celia Keenan-Bolger
(Tony Award for her role as Scout in *To Kill a Mockingbird* 2019)

CONCLUSION

"YOU CAN'T TEACH ACTING! YOU CAN'T TEACH ACTING!" a friend stated boldly and with complete self-assurance. But, in fact, I did...for 38 years. Was I on a fool's errand? "Can acting be learned?" is perhaps the deeper question, and to that I can say categorically, "Yes!" Steven Strait, a young actor in the TV series, *The Expanse,* was quoted regarding his training at the Stella Adler School of Acting, "For me, acting is a combination of empathy, intelligence, and vulnerability, and those three things can be worked on. What it did for me was to open me up... It scared me to death when I first got there. But...it was the act of jumping into it that I think allowed me to start learning how to use that tool and that instrument. I do think it's a skill that can be learned."

One of our undergraduate students from Wayne State, who had some success as an actor in Chicago, sent a Facebook message to the faculty members at Wayne: "You guys taught me so much!"

Marlon Brando, in his book *Songs My Mother Taught Me*, credited Stella Adler with teaching him acting. It can be learned. Examples abound. No, you can't make someone into a great actor, but you can offer him some foundational techniques.

And what about my own learning as I taught acting over the years? Most of that I've tried to set down in these pages. It was an evolution from lots of time spent on lengthy relaxation and improvisational exercises, to more time spent on scripted work, though not exclusively so. The evolution never stopped. I found joy in the search to keep making it better, and I think that came out of my passion for the craft, and how I might offer ways to go for those who wished to learn it. It became my goal to teach measurable, core skills that were immediately useful for the acting students. In the end, it's what the students can do or not do that's the measurement of teaching success.

I would add that teaching is also a skill, and like any skill, it takes some time to develop. It's not merely being a critic. It's far more than that. It's easy to get puffed up by student praise, particularly from the younger students. It's easy to revel in student success in improvs and exercises and to lose sight of the fact that these are often secondary tools for their toolboxes.

And ultimately, I think you, teacher, must admit that there is not one way to teach acting. There are many approaches to learning this exciting, challenging craft. The older actors' response to our young apprentice questions about "The Method" was, "If it works for you, fine." Colm Feore, that sensational leading man with the Canadian Stratford Theatre Festival, said that when he was in training at the Canadian National Theatre Academy, he took from each teacher the things that worked the best for him. He also mentioned that a big part of his learning came from watching the older pros at Stratford when he was a young actor there. Now, as a more seasoned one, he said, "It takes a long time to become a classical actor."

I offer this paradoxical statement, "Be prepared to be surprised," meaning that on some infrequent occasions, you, as teacher, are going to see a scene or monologue that will blow you away. It will come alive and absorb you totally. I recall a scene from the first act of *Cat on a Hot Tin Roof* between Maggie the Cat and Brick, in which the two actors simply nailed it big-time. I thought that they could have done it anywhere. I wanted to run up onstage when it was over and hug them, but I didn't out of respect for the other students in the class. It either comes alive or it doesn't, and that scene did, beautifully.

I was very, very lucky in my career as a teacher. For starters, I had many wonderful students who were talented, enthusiastic, open to learning, and curious about the craft. I felt very responsible to always give them my best work, be thoroughly prepared, and be open and responsive to their work. To be encouraging as well. We all need that. But their excitement, energy, and talent were a continual turn-on.

I also had very good teachers and mentors myself. Those inspiring professional actors in summer stock, who taught me through their work, which I was able to watch every night, and let it be absorbed into my system. Otto Kvapil at Xavier University, who introduced me to the classics, taught me how to cast and stage a play, and made the process of doing the work such a joy and so filled with laughter.

I had good leaders and bosses in every situation. J. Carter Rowland at Gannon College in Erie, Pennsylvania, Roy Bowen and John Morrow at The Ohio State University, Selden "Scotty" Faulkner at the University of Wisconsin-Stevens Point, Leonard Leone at Wayne State University in Detroit. Each one of them was encouraging and supportive. I also had terrific colleagues in each place where I worked, and I remember them with sheer thanks for their help, talent, and friendship.

Each of my working situations contributed mightily to the career growth I needed at the time. At Gannon College, I was given a theatre, a few courses to teach, and the freedom to learn from my mistakes and successes as I directed and taught. At Ohio State, where I did my graduate work, my eyes were opened to a whole new depth of theatre history, literature, and production. At the University of Wisconsin-Stevens Point, I was given the acting classes to teach, and the freedom to learn and grow and to develop my own approach to acting instruction, as well as to grow in my directing work. At Wayne State University, I was given the opportunity to do lots of directing and teaching of acting on the graduate level and the undergraduate as well.

I would be totally remiss in extending thanks if I did not mention the great gift that the aforementioned student at the University of Wisconsin-Stevens Point, Richard Gustin, gave me when he recommended me to Leonard Leone and Wayne State. From that came a huge step forward in my career, and I will be forever grateful to Dick for his support.

And thanks again, to Chris Bohan, whose first email asking for, "any advice to a novice teacher," propelled me on the road to this work. I know he has used some of it and then added his own talent to it, as he continues to find the way that works best for him. We all eventually find our own way to go as we grow from experience.

I've had a great ride in all this. I had dream jobs and never felt like I ever was "going to work," but rather couldn't wait to get there and continue the process. I mentioned at the start of these pages that my goal in all of this was twofold. One was to share with beginning teachers of acting, and maybe some vets too, some ways to go that eventually worked for me. It took me some time to develop these approaches, and if another teacher can find them useful, I will feel like I have succeeded. I hope and believe that this book can be useful for the actor as well. The grounding in a doable action and the techniques that follow can be a workable path forward if the actor chooses to take it.

For all of you, I can only wish that you find the joy, excitement, and fulfillment that I found as I pursued this wonderful work. For the teacher and the actor, you have chosen a very special path. May your journey be filled with a special energy that only you can know. Bless you all.

Nicholas Nickleby at the Hilberry Theatre 1988.
How it came to be.

I believe that Leonard Leone first suggested that the Hilberry Company do *Nicholas Nickleby* after he saw the Royal Shakespeare performance on Broadway, and I believe that he whispered his idea into Howard Burman's ear. It was decided to put *Nicholas Nickleby* into the 1987-88 Hilberry Theatre Season as the sixth and seventh shows. A few adjustments had to be made to accommodate the normal rotating repertory rehearsal and performance schedule, and this was done by the more-than-capable Margaret Spear, Theatre Management and Marketing Director. I can still hear her counting out the rehearsals. Tony Schmitt was assigned to direct it.
  When it came time to plan and hold auditions, the reality of the project took hold. One of the graduate stage/theatre managers, Daniel Ziegler, offered to be the production manager. He set up butcher block paper in a classroom (across a wall) and listed all the actors and all the parts on a chart. The play required 41 actors to play 290 parts. These characters and the narrators were all listed on the chart. Casting began. It took five days. 20 Hilberry Graduate Repertory Company actors and 21 undergraduate student actors and a few Ph.D. students were cast. Only five roles were single cast; everyone else was (at least) double and triple cast.
  The set was designed by Russell Smith, Director of Scenic Design; the lighting by new Lighting Designer Thomas Schraeder; and the overwhelming job of designing all the costumes fell to Hilberry Costume Designer, Robin ver Hage. Tony immediately knew that he would need help with the directing; two other graduate stage managers/directing majors, James Baird and Vincent Scott, directed various story lines. Then there was the music. Another graduate theatre management/directing major, Roger Bean, offered to take charge. He convinced the chair to provide synthesized music, and then he taught the music to the cast.
  It was a challenging couple of months. Rehearsals were held in three different spaces (most in the old church), and then suddenly it was opening night. The schedule was such that Part One opened on Holy Thursday and Part Two on Good Friday, with both parts playing in the afternoon and evening on the day before Easter! We walked over to the theatre on Holy Thursday wondering how many

people would come. We were surprised to see so many cars in the parking lot. Then, as we walked over again on Good Friday, we were even more surprised.

My most favorite memory, perhaps of my over 25 years of Hilberry shows, is of when the lights came up at the beginning of Part Two on Friday evening. Part One ends with the cast in a tableau, and Part Two begins with that same tableau. As the lights came up on the cast, the audience stood up and applauded! We were overwhelmed!

The shows played to sold-out houses with an additional performance added. Our audiences talked about it for many years. Even though Tony doesn't reference the show in his book, it will always be a wonderful memory and an amazing accomplishment for the Hilberry Theatre. I felt it should be documented.

--JBMS

(Photo courtesy of Wayne State University Photo Services, Patricia Clay photographer)

SOME BOOKS I FOUND USEFUL AND INSPIRING

There are many good books on acting, but here are some that influenced me. Many of them are older books, but at the time of this writing, are still available from Amazon.

An Actor Prepares by Constantin Stanislavski...The foundational book of modern acting. Sir Michael Redgrave said that he read it every year despite some of his friends kidding him about it.

Audition by Michael Shurtleff... His "Twelve Guideposts of Acting" are very practical, and they reflect the point of view of a man who as a casting director came to some conclusions about the craft. His analysis of scene work is very insightful and helpful for the actor.

A Practical Handbook for the Actor by Melissa Bruder, et. al. ... Acting students of David Mamet and Bill Macey stress the need for essential action as the basis of acting. Their "nine qualities of a good action" are an important guide for the actor.

Playing Shakespeare by John Barton... The first chapter on "the two traditions" is so clear and illustrative of honest acting, especially its view of "playing a quality." There is a DVD of his workshop in which he uses top actors from the Royal Shakespeare Company.

Being an Actor by Simon Callow... The original Mozart in *Amadeus* tells much about the process of acting through stories of personal experience. Callow is clearly an actor who has reflected on the process of acting, and he has communicated it in this and other books he has written.

Letters from an Actor by William Redfield... An actor who is playing Guildenstern in Richard Burton's *Hamlet*, writes a series of letters to a friend describing the daily happenings in rehearsals and his impression of them. Many insightful comments on acting, from an actor who knew his craft.

Strasberg at the Actors Studio by Robert H. Hethmon... The author tape-recorded many classes that Strasberg taught. I found it truly revealing and in contrast to the many comments that I had heard or read about this iconic teacher. Lots of useful information and exercises.

Songs My Mother Taught Me by Marlon Brando... Brando talks at some length about acting, and how much he learned from Stella Adler, whom he credits with literally changing how acting changed in America.

About Acting by Peter Barkworth... A British West End actor and head of the Royal Academy of Dramatic Art lays out his very practical techniques of acting. He has a lengthy chapter of exercises, useful for teacher and actor.

A Challenge for the Actor by Uta Hagen... This master actor and teacher brings her wealth of experience to her approach to the craft. Many practical and solid techniques, and lots of exercises. I heard her say, "Don't get my earlier book, *Respect for Acting*. That's crap! Get my new book, *A Challenge for the Actor*!"

Actors on Acting by Toby Cole and Helen Krich Chinoy... A compendium of actors throughout the ages starting with Greece and Rome up to our contemporary ones. Biographical sketches but primarily what the major players had to say about their craft. A lengthy but good reference book.

Acting is Believing by Charles McGaw... A practical working of some of the principles that Stanislavski set down in *An Actor Prepares*. Good exercise work in it. Sound technical principles. Good for the teacher as well as the actor.

Actors Talk About Acting by Lewis Funk and John E. Booth... Interviews of prominent actors. An older book and surprisingly still available through Amazon. I'm sure there are many more current books like this, but I really want to know what the likes of John Gielgud, Lynne Fontaine, Maureen Stapleton, Helen Hayes, and many others have to say about what they do. I am fascinated by the fact that Anne Bancroft took a ride on a roller coaster blindfolded to prepare to do *The Miracle Worker* to get the feeling of helplessness that Helen Keller must have felt. I love stories like that.

Voice and Speech for the Theatre by J. Clifford Turner... The voice teacher at the Royal Academy of Dramatic Art lays out his dicta and exercises for vocal production. An invaluable book on this topic.

Act One by Moss Hart... Hart's rise to success by watching what George Kaufman and the audience were telling him about making a play work on the stage.

How Not to Write a Play by Walter Kerr... A book I read when I was a senior in high school, and one that formed a great deal of my own aesthetic and still does.

Books also mentioned:

Ellen Terry's Memoirs by Ellen Terry

Improvisation for the Theatre by Viola Spolin

Training an Actor by Sonia Moore

The Michael Chekhov Handbook for the Actor by Lenard Petit

In Spite of Myself by Christopher Plummer

Credits
Production Photographs: Wayne State University
Photo Services Department Photographers: Rick Beilaczyc, George Booth, Patricia Clay, Mary Jane Murawka;
Xavier University and The Ohio State University newspapers
About the Author and Back Cover Photographs: Lara Anne Salter, Salter Photography
Cover Design: Robert J. Medici

Authors:
Edward Albee, *Who's Afraid of Virginia Woolf*
Frances Goodrich and Albert Hackett, *The Diary of Anne Frank*; adapted from the book *The Diary of a Young Girl* by Anne Frank
George Bernard Shaw, *Misalliance*
John Steinbeck, *Of Mice and Men*
All with permission from Dramatists Play Service

Professionals quoted:
Actors from the Stratford and Shaw Theatre Festivals in Canada: Colm Feore, Marti Maraden, Barry McGregor, Nicholas Pennell. New York-based Voice Specialist Clive Vinson

ACKNOWLEDGMENTS

I know that Tony would like to acknowledge the many people he talked to about this work over the several years that he worked on this book. His first acknowledgment would go to John R. Gutting, Ph.D., a long-time friend, fellow actor at Xavier University, a teacher, director and writer, who edited this book in its several iterations over the years. John's time and energy, vision and suggestions helped to hone the book into what it is. He did final edits with me after Tony passed, and I especially thank him for that.

He would thank the many former students that he contacted for their impressions of his teaching and directing, as well as their current thoughts on both. Some, but probably not all, include, from Gannon College: Sheila Hickey Garvey, Thomas Nardone, Barbara Root Seyler, Anthony Walley; from University of Wisconsin-Stevens Point: Richard Gustin, Kathy Kinney; from Wayne State University: Alan Litsey, Jordan Whalen, Barbara Tarbuck, and, of course Christopher Bohan, many of whom read either various chapters or the whole book and gave Tony feedback. A special thanks to Tony's Wayne State University Department of Theatre colleague, Movement Specialist Nira Pullin, who offered editing, insight, and clarifying ideas.

My special thanks to graphic designer and the best neighbor ever, Robert Medici, for proofreading, helping me with some of the photos and especially for designing and executing the cover of this book. Finally, I will be ever grateful to Tony's cousin Barbara Koch for her enthusiasm, her time and skills in proofreading and editing, and for creating the Index for the final version of this book.

Tony would thank his (some as noted earlier) teachers, department chairs and mentors: Otto Kvapil at Xavier University; Robert Butler, Chair, at St. Louis University; J.

Carter Rowland and John Rouch, Chairs, at Gannon College; John Morrow and Roy Bowen, Chair, at The Ohio State University; Seldon (Scotty) Faulkner, Chair, at the University of Wisconsin-Stevens Point; Leonard Leone, Howard Burman, Robert Hazzard, James Thomas and Blair V. Anderson, Chairs, at Wayne State University.

And I know Tony would also want to mention his colleagues William Leonard, Robert McGill, Nira Pullin, Russell Smith, Thomas Schraeder, Larry Kaushansky, Mary Copenhagen, Fred Florkowski, Mary Pratt Cooney, Nancy Lipschultz, Edward Smith, Cynthia Blaise, Martin Molson, Alice Faust, Susan Hunt Hagen, James Moore, and the many others with whom he worked and shared ideas daily.

I think he would also thank me for finishing the book! He would thank our children, Steve, Vickie, and Tony, who, growing up over the years, acquiesced more than once to his schedule of many rehearsals and productions. We often said we couldn't have done what we did, especially at Wayne State, if we didn't have the best children in the world!

Finally, as he notes in his Conclusion, he would want to thank all the students and actors with whom he worked over the years. He would want you to know that you have each contributed to his growth and love of his work.

--JBMS

Steve Schmitt
Stop the World I Want to Get Off
(directed by Seldon Faulkner)
University of Wisconsin-Stevens Point

Tony Schmitt, Mark Corkins
A Christmas Carol
Bonstelle Theatre
Wayne State University

Vickie and Steve Schmitt in *Medea*
(directed by Alice Faust)
University of Wisconsin-Stevens Point

John Gutting, Jerry Simon, Tony Schmitt
The Doctor in Spite of Himself
Xavier University

Tony Schmitt and John Gutting
Xavier University

Tony Schmitt and Tom Nardone
Gannon College

About the Author

Anthony (Tony) Schmitt spent 25 years at Wayne State University's Department of Theatre, in Detroit, Michigan, teaching and directing at its Hilberry, Bonstelle and Studio Theatres.

Tony was the Associate Director for Performance in charge of the 20-member Hilberry Graduate Repertory Theatre Acting Company and Program. He directed over 70 productions at Wayne State, including the Best Director and Best Play Award-winning *Nicholas Nickleby*. He received Theatre Excellence Award nominations from the *Detroit Free Press*, *The Detroit News* and the *Oakland Press* for his productions of *Amadeus, Equus, The Grapes of Wrath* and *The Heidi Chronicles* at the Hilberry Theatre, as well as *A Moon for the Misbegotten* at the Attic Theatre. His productions at the Bonstelle Theatre include *Cabaret, Cat Among the Pigeons, A Christmas Carol,* and *The Elephant Man*. During that time, Tony also directed *Noises Off* with Joyce DeWitt and Pat Paulson, and *Sleuth* with Noel Harrison at the Cherry County Playhouse, and *Romeo and Juliet* at the Utah Shakespearean Festival.

Tony began his theater education in Cincinnati, Ohio, as an apprentice at the Cincinnati Summer Playhouse where he appeared in productions with Luther Adler, Lois Smith, Robert Middleton, and Vivian Blaine. He has degrees from Xavier University (B.S.), St. Louis University (M.A.) and The Ohio State University (Ph.D.). Tony served as a Lieutenant in the U.S. Army, and also taught and/or directed at Gannon College in Erie, Pennsylvania, at The Ohio State University, at Otterbein College, at the University of Wisconsin-Stevens Point and the University of Richmond in London, England.

After his retirement, Tony served as Artistic Advisor for Meadow Brook Theatre where he directed *Witness for the Prosecution;* he directed *Twelfth Night* for Water Works Theatre's Shakespeare in the Park, and returned to the Hilberry as a Professor Emeritus to direct *Misalliance, Of Mice and Men,* and *Side Man* among others. He also returned to his love of writing, creating a play version of *The Scarlet Letter* that was produced in Birmingham, Alabama, and at the Oklahoma Shakespeare Festival.

Until Tony died in 2018, he and his wife Jan lived in Royal Oak, Michigan. They have three children, Stephen, Victoria and Anthony, and five grandchildren, Andrew (Drew), Brendan, Colin, Cayden, and Anthony (Cai).

Anthony Schmitt was a member of the Dramatists Guild, the Screen Actors Guild and the Society of Stage Directors and Choreographers.

In Praise of Tony Schmitt

Tony could cover the spectrum. He just understood theater—all the different facets. That's what made him a really good director. He was very versatile and knowledgeable. *Blair V. Anderson, Ph.D., Professor Emeritus, Wayne State University*

I think of him and his work and I think of depth and honesty and no baloney. You can tell when someone loves his art. *Lawrence Devine, Theatre Critic, Detroit Free Press*

Wayne State University
Detroit Michigan 48202

Office of the President
(313) 577-2230

April 5, 1990

Professor Anthony Schmitt
Theatre Department
College of Fine, Performing,
   and Communication Arts
200 95 W. Hancock
CAMPUS

Dear Tony:

This is the season of legislative activity, and many of my other activities fall far behind. For more than a month I have shifted back and forth on my desk a reminder to write you about that exceptional production of "Execution of Justice."

I took several friends, including two lawyers, and all raved about the message of the play, the forcefulness of its acting, the excellence of direction and production, and the use of courtroom scenes interspersed with dialogue and film to carry the message.

I personally was moved by your presentation of this play. Its injustice strikes home for many in our society. The Hilberry was courageous to present this play, and your direction gave it life and power.

Thanks again for giving us an excellent evening of theatre and a powerful message about injustice still rampant in our society.

Sincerely,

David Adamany
President

From His Students

It was always a joy to work with him....and time to talk in the sometime confusing world of theater and school. He really was one of the good directors who got the results in a pleasant room. *John Pribyl, M.F.A., Actor: Oregon Shakespeare Festival; American Players Theatre*

Tony sold me on repertory theatre and gave me the single best, direct, useful scene study question I still use as an actor: "Seriously, if you don't like the other character in the scene, no good reason for being there, why don't you just leave?" *Erik Gratton, M.F.A., Actor: Goodspeed Musicals,* Buddy the Elf *at Madison Square Garden*

Tony was a beautiful, bright, funny, talented, patient, kind, supportive and insightful man, a nurturing teacher, and an incisive director. *Jennifer Tuttle, M.F.A., Assistant Professor and Director at City University of New York*

Tony was an incredible teacher to me...*Sean Allan Krill, Actor: Broadway,* Jagged Little Pill, Mama Mia

He made me a better actor because he gave me the confidence that I had all the creativity I needed inside of me. *Roxanne Wellington, M.F.A., Actor, Instructor at The Dobbins Conservatory of Theatre and Dance at Southeast Missouri State University.*

He forever will have an impact on me as an actor, director, teacher; he was the mentor I needed. *Jordan Whalen, M.F.A., Actor: Regional Theatre; TV-*Becoming Royal

I remember his keen direction in class scenes and plays I acted in. *Camille Price, M.F.A., Actor*

He changed my life. He allowed me the opportunity to discover courage that was just lurking there waiting to be discovered. *Diane Bailiff, Ph.D., Professor, Emporia State University*

No other director I've worked with has been as unfailingly encouraging and supportive. He convinced you that you could be better...and you became better because of his support and encouragement. *Tony Dobrowolski, M.F.A., Actor: Artistic Associate at the Shakespeare Project of Chicago; Chicago Shakespeare*

He had a way of honestly telling you like it is when directing you that would encourage and not crush you. *Lindsay Stuart Worth, B.F.A., Actor, film, TV*

There are no greater gifts in life than those bestowed by a true mentor. I will carry forward his teaching, his thoughtful suggestion, and his willingness to help a young man so in need of wisdom. Much of who I am today is because of who he was. *Phillip Walter Moss, Ph.D., Faculty, Director, University Liggett School, Grosse Pointe, Michigan; Michigan Thespian Society.*

Tony taught me the importance of three core sentences in every scene: What do you want? What happens if you don't get it? Why don't you just leave? *Kristopher Yoder, M.F.A., Actor, Teacher*

He was an absolutely brilliant teacher and director; ...as he taught it, the art of acting is about getting in touch with the very essence of the human experience. *Karen Vincent Humiston, B.F.A., Actor, Researcher*

His acting instruction was never filled with superfluous, pointless direction. At its core, it was about knowing what your character was "doing." He made me want to be a better actor and a better person. I catch myself repeating many of his words of wisdom to my own students daily. *Mike Schraeder, Ph.D., Director/Chair of Acting at KD Studio and Conservatory of Film and Dramatic Arts, Dallas, Texas*

And such a great director! ...and it was so much fun to be directed by him! I can still hear him laughing*!!! Julie Levo, M.A., Actor, Program Director at New York Medical College.*

INDEX

Note: Italicized page numbers indicate photographs.

A
Abbott, George, 93–94
Abelard and Heloise (Millar), 85–86, *142*
Act One (Hart), 15
Acting, ability to learn, 179
Acting, goal of, 11, 43–44, 173–174
Acting is Believing (McGaw), 16
Action, 27–37
    defined, 27–28
    examples, 28–32, 36–37
    exercises, 31–32
    importance of, 33–34
    traps and dangers, 34–35
Actor Prepares (Stanislavski), 15–16, 156, 157, 167
Adamany, David, 195
Adcock, Anne, *176*
Adler, Luther, 11, 57
Akey, William, *143*
Alexander, LeWan, *176*
Ali, Mahershala, 109–111
All Over Town (Schisgal), 165, *176*
Anastasia (Maurette), 12
Anderson, Blair V., 190, 195, back cover
Anderson, Judith, 12
Arms and the Man (Shaw), 69
As Time Goes By, 83–84
Audience, communicating with, 15, 53, 131, 152–153, 165–166
Audition (Shurtleff), 19, 57, 165, 167, 172
Auntie Mame (Lawrence and Lee), *143*
Ayers, David, *25*

B
Bailiff, Diane, 196
Baird, James, 183
Baker, Brenda, *176*
Barton, John, 131
Bean, Roger, 183

199

Bedford, Brian, 110
Bening, Annette, 34, 63
Betrayal (Pinter), 47
Black Chiffon (Storm), 12
Blaise, Cynthia, 190
Bohan, Chris, 9, 41, *177*, 182, 189
Books, recommended, 185–188
Bowen, Roy, 190
Brando, Marlon, 81, 179
Breathing, 118–119, 122–123
"Bringing it alive," 73–75
Budzinski, Richard, *89*
Burman, Howard, 183, 190
Butler, Robert, 189

C
Cabaret, *176*
Callow, Simon, 43
Capote, 94
Cariou, Len, 125
Cat Among the Pigeons (Feydeau), *176*
Character, 68–69, 109–116
    defining, 110–112
    exercises, 114–115
    judgment of, 69
    physicality and, 113
    vocal quality and, 113
Chekhov, Michael, 17
Chemin de Fer (Feydeau), *143*
Chorus Line, 86
Chorus of Disapproval (Ayckbourn), 43
Christmas Carol (Dickens), 60
Cincinnati Summer Playhouse, 10–13, *24*
Cole (Porter), *176*
Communication, 51–55
concentration, 157–158
Cook, Kim, *89*
Cooney, Mary Pratt, 190
Copenhagen, Mary, 190
Corkins, Mark, *89*
Courtenay, Tom, 113
Cramer, Doug, 11

D
Dammerall, Elizabeth, *24*
Danner, Blythe, 47
Delicate Balance (Albee), *142*
Dench, Judi, 62, 83–84, 146
DePinto, Nick, *177*
Diary of Anne Frank (Goodrich and Hackett), *89*
    action, 28, 32, 36, 129–130
    character, 111, 112
    imagination, 84
    inflection, 132
    observation, 95
    obstacle, 39, 49
    real life, 68, 69–70
    scene partner, connecting with, 57
    story, sense of, 98–99
Diction, 125–127
Dobrowolski, Tony, 197
Doherty, Antonette, *142*
Domutz, Duane, *89*
Dozier, Cynthia, *143*
Dreyfuss, Richard, 120
Duse, Eleonora, 70

E
Eccentricities of a Nightingale (Williams), 49–50, *89*
Elder, Mary, *143*
Ellen Terry's Memoirs (Terry), 66
Emotion, 77–86, 150–151
    depth of, 84–86
    and imagination, 80, 82
    need for, 77–80
    script and, 81
    techniques, 80–84
Empty Space (Brook), 61
Equus (Shaffer), 55
Exercises
    action, 31–32
    breathing, 122–123
    communication, 53–55
    concentration, 157–158
    diction, 127
    imagination, 71–72

listening, 54–55
loosening up, 147–151, 159–160
observation, 45–46, 130–131
obstacle, 45–46, 49
opening up to partner, 61–63
physicality, 138–139
relaxation, 121, 156–157
sensory awareness, 161–162
teaching of, 17
voice, 121–123

F
Faulkner, Selden "Scotty," 181, 190, *191*
Faust, Alice, 190, *191*
Fences (Wilson), 165–166
Feore, Colm, 110, 180
Ference, Mary Ann, *89*
Ferrer, Jose, 81
Five Easy Pieces, 83
Florkowski, Fred, *177,* 190
Frank, Anne. See *Diary of Anne Frank*
Freeing the Natural Voice (Linklater), 119

G
Garrick, David, 93
Garvey, Sheila Hickey, 189
Gielgud, John, 81, 94
Glass Menagerie (Williams), *25, 59,* 172
Graczyk, Edward, *25*
Grapes of Wrath (Steinbeck), *177*
Gratton, Erik, *142,* 196
Gustin, Richard, 6, 19, *88, 143,* 182, 189
Guthrie, Tyrone, 20, 69, 146
Gutting, John R., 189, *191*
Guys and Dolls (Loesser), 113, *176*

H
Hagen, Susan Hunt, 190
Hagen, Uta, 17, 44, 136, 169–170, 172
Hasso, Signe, 12
Hazzard, Robert, 190
Helpmann, Max, 84–85
Henry V (Shakespeare), 65

Hoffman, Philip Seymour, 95
Hopkins, Anthony, 55
How to Succeed in Business (Loesser), *88*
Humiston, Karen Vincent, 197, back cover

I
Imagination, 65–75
    actors' experiences, 65–66
    bringing it alive, 73–75
    character and, 68–71
    emotion and, 80, 82
    exercises, 71–72
    in real life, 67–68
Importance of Being Earnest (Wilde), 18, *24*
Improvisation, 61, 150–151, 163–164
In Spite of Myself (Plummer), 65, 66
Inflection, 132–133

J
Jackson, Charles, *176*
Jones, Erman, *142*

K
Kadish, Lynne, *142*
Kass, Peter, 73
Keenan-Bolger, Celia, *177*
King Lear (Shakespeare), 93
Kinney, Kathy, 189
Krill, Sean Allan, 196
Kvapil, Otto, 14–15, *24*, 111, 181, 189

L
La La Land, 79, 86
Lady of Larkspur Lotion (Williams), 12
Langham, Michael, 53
Language, music of, 129–134
Leonard, William, 190
Leone, Leonard, 181, 182, 190
Liar (Goldoni), 40
Lipschultz, Nancy, 190
Linklater, Kristen, 119
Listening, 54–55
Litsey, Alan, 189

Lonergan, Kenneth, 173–174
Loosening up, 145–153, 159–160
Lover (Pinter), 37

M
MacGregor, Barry, 43, 152–153
MacLiammoir, Micheal, 92
Manchester by the Sea, 173–174
Maraden, Marti, 152, 153
Mason, Brewster, 72
Maxwell, Jan, 78
McGaw, Charles, 16
McGill, Robert, 190
McKellen, Ian, 117, 131
Measure for Measure (Shakespeare), 110
Medici, Robert, 2, 188, 189
Merchant of Venice (Shakespeare), 131
Merkerson, S. Epatha, 20
Method acting, 66, 81, 180
Millard, Peter, 79
Misalliance (Shaw), 51–52, 116, *177*
Mister Abbott (Abbott), 93–94
Molson, Martin, 190
Monologue, inner, 43–50
Monroe, Maribeth, *176*
Moore, Aaron, *177*
Moore, James, 190
Moore, Sonia, 17, 47
Morrow, John, 94, 181, 190
Moss, Phillip Walter, 197
My Fair Lady (Lerner and Loewe), *25,* 81

N
Nardone, Thomas, 6, 189, *191*
Nicholas Nickleby (Dickens), 183–184, *184*
Nichols, Mike, 59, 97, 146
Nicholson, Jack, 83
Night Thoreau Spent in Jail (Lawrence and Lee), *25,* 83
Notes, 168–172

O
Observation, 33, 45–46, 91–95, 130–131
Obstacle, 39–42, 49–50, 165

Of Mice and Men (Steinbeck), *142*
   character, 111–113
   communication, 53
   emotion, 81
   imagination, 70–71
   scene partner, connecting with, 58
   sensory awareness, 160
   story, sense of, 99–107
Olivier, Lawrence, 69
On the Waterfront, 81
Openness to partner, 60–63
Our Town (Wilder), 36, 41, 74, *89,* 113, 136–137

P
Pennell, Nicholas, 45, 92, 118
Performance sense, 165–166
Phillips, Robin, 152
Physicality, 135–140, 166
Pinter, Harold, 133–134
Playing Shakespeare (Barton), 131
Plummer, Christopher, 65, 66
Practical Handbook for the Actor (Bruder), 19
Pribyl, John, 196
Proposition, 79
Prouty, Peter, *142*
Pullin, Nira, *176,* 189, 190

Q
Quintero, Jose, 107

R
Real life, 51–52, 61, 67–70, 80, 86. *See also* Observation
Regionalisms (diction), 126
Relaxation, 156–157
Robinson, Smokey, 163–164
Romeo and Juliet (Shakespeare), 37, 70, 84–85, 107–108
Rouch, John, 189
Rowland, J. Carter, 181, 189
Royal Family (Kaufman and Ferber), 78

S
Saint Joan (Shaw), 40
Santiago-Hudson, Ruben, 20

Scene partner, connecting with, 57–63
    examples, 58–59
    exercises, 61–63, 149
    importance of, 57
    openness and vulnerability, 60–63
Scheider, Roy, 47
Schmitt, Anthony (Tony), *24, 25*
    apprenticeship, 10–13
    Gannon College, 15–16
    Hilberry Theatre Company, 19–20, 183–184
    mentors, 13, 14, 181
    Ohio State University, 16
    St. Louis University, 14–15
    teaching career, 17–22, 179–182, 191–192
    University of Wisconsin-Stevens Point, 17
    Wayne State University, 19–20
    Xavier University, 13–14
Schmitt, Andrew (Drew), 194
Schmitt, Anthony (Cai), 194
Schmitt, Brendan, 194
Schmitt, Colin, 194
Schmitt, Cayden, 194
Schmitt, Janet Barrett Moore (Jan), 6, 184, 190, 194
Schmitt, Steve, 190, *191*, Stephen, 194
Schmitt, Tony B., 190, *191*, Anthony, 192
Schmitt, Vickie, *176,* 190, *191,* Victoria, 192
Schraeder, Mike, 197, back cover
Schraeder, Thomas, 183
Scott, Vincent, 183
Sensory awareness, 160–162
Servant of Two Masters (Goldoni), *88*
Seyler, Barbara Root, 189
Shakespeare, William, 53, 72, 92, 131, 140
She Stoops to Conquer (Goldsmith), 113
Shurtleff, Michael, 19, 57, 59, 165, 167, 172
Side Man (Leight), *177*
Sikorski, Katie, *89*
Skinner, Edith, 123–124, 127
Smith, Lois, 12, *24*
Smith, Russell, *143,* 183, 190
Somerville, Phyllis, 20, 170
Spear, Margaret, 183
Spolin, Viola, 17

St. Joan (Shaw), *143*
Stanislavski, Constantin, 15–16, 17, 110, 117, 156, 167
Stapleton, Maureen, 12
Stone, Emma, 79, 86
Story, sense of, 97–108
Strasberg, Lee, 17
Streep, Meryl, 77–78, 146
Substitution, 66, 81
Suda, Thomas M., *176*

T
Tale of Two Cities (Dickens), *142*
Taming of the Shrew (Shakespeare), 13, *24,* 67, 125
Tambor, Jeffrey, 20
Tandy, Jessica, 79
Tarbuck, Barbara, 20, 189
Tarrant, Jean, *25*
Terminology, 167
Terry, Ellen, 65–66, 82
20th Century Women, 63
Thomas, James, 190
Tolar, Dwight, *142*
Tomlin, Lily, 20
Training an Actor (Moore), 47
Turner, J. Clifford, 118, 127
Tuttle, Jennifer, 164

U
Umland, Ken, *142*
Uncle Vanya (Chekhov), 59

V
ver Hage, Robin, 183
View from the Bridge (Miller), 11, 57
Vilanche, Bruce, *25*
Vinson, Clyde, 120
Voice, 117–124
    ability to learn, 118, 124
    and breathing, 118–119
    exercises, 121–123
    importance of, 117
    mental aspects, 120
Voice and Speech in Theatre (Turner), 118

W
Walley, Anthony, 189
Wayne, John, 55
Wellington, Roxanne, 196
Whalen, Jordan, 189, 196
Who's Afraid of Virginia Woolf? (Albee), 125–126
Widowers' Houses (Shaw), 79
Williams, Cheryl, *176*
Williams, Michelle, 173–174
Worth, Lindsay Stuart, 197
Wright, Max, 20

Y
Yoder, Kristopher, 197, back cover
Young and Beautiful (Benson), 12, *24*

Z
Ziegler, Daniel, 183

Made in the USA
Columbia, SC
18 November 2020